How to Write Your Book
(Guaranteed!)

How to Write Your Book (Guaranteed!)

Thomas A. Williams, PhD

WILLIAMS & COMPANY
BOOK PUBLISHERS

ISBN 978-1-878853-93-6

LCCN 2005905733

Printed in the United States of America

Williams & Company, Book Publishers
1317 Pine Ridge Drive
Savannah, Georgia 31406
Bookpub@Comcast.Net

For the Richardson Girls,

Madeleine, Anna and Currin,

who will write the next great books!

Also by Thomas A. Williams

Mallarmé and the Language of Mysticism

Eliphas Lévi: Master of the Tarot, the Cabala, and the Secret Doctrines

The Bicentennial Book

We Choose America

The Query Letter That Never Fails

Tales of the Tobacco Country

Poet Power: The Complete Guide to Getting Your Poetry Published

How to Publish Weekly Newspapers and Free Circulation Shoppers

How to Publish City and Regional Magazines

The Self-Publisher's Handbook of Contacts and Sources

How to Make $100,000 a Year in Desktop Publishing

Publiash Your Own Magazine, Guidebook or Weekly Newspaper

Get Paid to Write!

TABLE OF CONTENTS

To the Reader   9

This book is for you if you want to write a book, but don't know how; or if you have to write a book but don't know how; or if you are so confused about it all you aren't sure what you know • Empowering yourself

1 / How I Discovered My Book Writing System   15

A Blue Horse notebook and a scripto pencil • A blank page stares me down • I wanted to write, but didn't know what to write or how • How I found myself in the position of having to write, whether I thought I could do it or not • The challenge of a dissertation • I discover a writing system that makes it easy • Start to finish in nine months • More books to come.

2 / Step One: Gathering the Tools   23

A few bucks and a trip to Office Depot will get you everything you need • It's the little things that count • Tempted by shortcuts? Don't take them.

3 / Step Two: Defining Your Master Idea   27

What is a Master Idea? • Your Master Idea is the organizing force • Some great Master Ideas, and why they worked • The magnet and the filings • Your Master Idea focuses your attention in a way that you have never experienced before • How to relenlessly attract ideas from every source in your sourroundings.

4 / Step Three: Taking Out the Garbage 37

We have had the imagination educated out of us • Overcoming all creative obstacles • How to accept snd enjoy your own creativity • Your mind is a 24 hour a day, non-stop idea factory — if you pay attention to it • How to cleanse your mind of all that hinders it • Breaking free to creativity.

5 / Step Four: Mind Harvesting 45

The closer you pay attention the more ideas you have • The evanescent nature of ideas and insights • Capturing ideas before they disappear • Using your pocket notebook • Reactions and enrichments • Respect your mind: it really is a miracle • How to overcome self-criticism

6 / Step Five: Creating Idea Slips 57

Ideas slips: the first step in storing and organizing ideas • How to make an idea slip • What goes on the slip? From pocket notebook to idea slip • From book margins to idea slips • Ideas and reactions to ideas

7 / Step Six: Creating Chapter Folders 65

Preparing Chapter Folders • Doing the spread and sorting the slips into the appropriate folder • Leaving a little leeway • A folder and what it contains • Organizing your folders for maximum effect

8 / Step Seven: Expanding Your Ideas 71

How to squeeze out the meaning — all of it • Every acorn contains an oak tree • Your own oak trees • It's in your mind — see it! • Mapping an idea tree and all its branches • How toexpand your insight, automatically

9/ The Horse's Mouth   **79**

A powerful way to enrich your book • How to get quotes no one else has • Get experts in the field to join with you in your project —they'll love it! • Why experts will collaborate with you • Sample letters and contact techniques

10 / Tips from an Old Pro's Toolkit   **87**

Grabbing (and holding) the reader's attention • Stylisic devices that let you do this • The ten second sort and the first five pages • How to handle quotes and direct discourse • Telling detail, and how to use them • The importance of transitions, and how to use them • The master pattern of non-fiction writing: the Freelancer's Paradigm

11 / Coda: Getting Published   **103**

Two ways to get published • How to approach trade publishers • The query letter, and how to write one • How to write a book proposal • How to publish it yourself • Why self-publishing is easily and inexpensively done • The digital printing revolution • What POD is and is not • Pitfalls to avoid when self-publishing

Appendix 1 / Contacts and Sources   **117**

Eight essential and one whimsical addition to your writing and publishing bookshelf • Magazines you should read and organizations you should join

Appendix 2 / Tom's Inside Publishing FAQ   **123**

The questions everybody wants answered, from how to get an agent to how to sell a book • The real skinny, no holds barred

Index   **165**

To the Reader

MY NAME IS TOM Williams, and I wrote this book for you. In doing so I assume that at least one of the following three things is true:

❏ You have a book idea in your head that's going to drive you crazy if you don't get it down on paper, but you don't know how to do it.

❏ You have some idea how to write your book, but find yourself struggling through a morass of disorganization, false starts and self-imposed limitations.

❏ You really don't want to write a book, but you don't have any choice. Whether you like it or not, you've got to sit down at your typewriter or computer and start hitting those keys.

—Perhaps your boss told you to write a company history;

—Or you have to write a thesis or dissertation to get your academic union card;

—Or you are a professional who needs a book to enhance your standing in your field;

—Or you need a book to sell in the back of the room at your seminars.

If you fall into any one of these categories, this book is for you. I was once in the very shoes that you are now wearing, those want-to-do-it-but-don't know-how shoes. Today, I can tell you that I have written and published fourteen non-fiction books. This is my fifteenth. The sixteenth is already in the on deck circle and ready to come up to bat. Many of my books are currently in print. Check me out at Amazon.com.

I have been published by university presses (University of Georgia Press and the University of Alabama Press), religious presses (Beka Books), major commercial publishers (F & W Books subsidiary, Betterway Publications), top-of-the line independent publishers (Sentient Publications), and I have self-published under my own imprints, Venture Press and Williams & Company, Book Publishers. I wrote my books while working full time at other jobs: teaching full-time in colleges and universities, creating and editing regional magazines and editing and publishing my own weekly newspaper.

I was able to do this because early on I developed a simple system that made it easy for me to do so. It will make it easy for you, too, and in the next 100 or so pages I share that system with you. The system is simple, and it works. This is what it will do for you:

❏ It will focus your attention as it has never been focused before.
❏ It will mine your every waking moment for creative ideas that you never even dreamed you had.

> My system will mine your every waking moment for creative ideas that you never even dreamed you had.

❏ It will teach you to collect these creative ideas, effortlessly, for inclusion in your book.

❏ It will spin out every last ounce of meaning that each of these ideas contains.

❏ It will organize your ideas into chapters for transcription into final book form.

All you have to do is *empower yourself* by following through, precisely, on the seven basic steps that make up my system. This rule holds for the smallest details. If I ask you to use a ball point pen, use one. If I recommend a pocket notebook of a certain size and type, get that notebook. If I ask you to use slips of paper cut to a certain size, don't ponder it, just do it.

The system is organic. Every part contributes to every other part. As the saying goes, trust me on this one. Just follow the rules, and the rest will take care of itself.

You will be amazed at how intelligent you have suddenly become, at how great ideas begin to leap into your mind unbidden, and how effortlessly you manage to put it all together when you sit down to write.

Does your mind feel like this when you sit down to write?

The 15th century alchemist Robert Fludd drew this fearsome representation of the primordial chaos that existed before the act of creation got to it and whipped it into shape. The Garden of Eden soon followed, every branch of every tree ripe with fruit. While I can't promise you a Garden of Eden, I can promise a simple method that makes it possible for you to tame your inner chaos, generate and collect the fruits of your mind, and mold them into the book you want to write.

· 1 ·

How I Discovered My Book Writing System

THE POPULATION OF THE known world is divided into two groups:

—Those who want to write a book, and don't,

—Those who want to write a book, and do.

There are a lot more people in the first group than in the second.

For years I was a frustrated member of Group One. I wanted to write a book but didn't know how. How do you start? I wondered. Where do your ideas come from? How do you fill up all the pages? How do you organize your effort so as to avoid sinking hopelessly beneath the surface of that perfect storm of details from which a book is made? It all seemed impossible, yet that was precisely what I longed to do.

When I was a child in rural South Georgia, my grandfather would give me a quarter on Saturday afternoons for helping with the chores. I remember walking down the red clay, pine-forested road to Shorty Wyant's general store (the same place my mother would take me to buy my Easter shoes) and buy a Blue Horse notebook and a Scripto mechanical pencil. I liked to hold and look at the Scripto. You could see through the transparent body and observe the inner workings of the helix-like silver shaft that twisted the lead up and down through the point.

I liked holding the notebooks, too. The covers were a shiny blue, and stiff. On the front was a drawing of a handsome horse, its collar on and ready for real work. The notebooks were sewn together on the spine, giving them an air of permanence. Like a book, I thought.

I also liked them because they had tables of equivalences printed on their back cover containing strange, melodious words like *avoirdupois*. Avoirdupois! How I loved that word. Even today it can conjure up the feelings and ambitions that danced though my mind as I walked home again up that country road with my Blue Horse in one hand and my mechanical pencil at the ready in the other.

But it also conjures up that strange, puzzled feeling that came upon me when I would later open the notebook and stare at that first, blank page. What was I supposed to write on it? How would I fill it up? And once the first page was done, what would I put on the second page, and the third, and all the pages after that?

I would like to tell you that I was a child prodigy and that I began to write flawless, balanced prose almost at once. But of course I did not. That blank page was too much for me. I gave up my literary ambitions and made a scrapbook of newspaper clippings about Rommel's advance across North Africa, which was taking place at the time. I knew in my heart I was supposed to write a book. It was my destiny! I just didn't know how to do it, and I had nobody to tell me.

The stand-off between me and that notebook—and many others like it—went on for years. There were school projects to struggle through. The simplest term paper assignment loomed before me like some literary Mt. Everest that I would have to surmount in the process of clawing my way up from the low-lands of English 101 to the slightly higher plane of English 102. I would type out everything important that I thought I knew, say, about the influence of steam power on the industrial revolution. Typically, that would require about three paragraphs. Getting beyond those paragraphs to the requisite ten or twelve pages was sheer torture.

I bought a Blue Horse notebook like this one to serve my budding literary ambitions, Instead, it became a scrapbook of newspaper clippings.

The standoff ends

But somehow I finished those papers and passed my courses. I continued moving on up the ladder of academe until I finally reached that supreme test for the literarily inhibited, the fearful *doctoral dissertation.*

I was at the University of North Carolina, a teaching assistant in the Department of Romance Languages. Stories of the heroic deeds of other graduate students struggling to wring an acceptable dissertation out of their battered psyches were prime topics of conversation in the stuffy little offices that we teaching assistants inhabited, each behind his single, tiny desk.

"It took Marvin five years, but he finally did it," someone would say.

"Well," another would counter, "Pete worked on his for eight years and finally gave it up. His credits expired. He would have had to start taking his course work all over again."

And there were dire stories of other dissertationless souls who wandered out into the Orange County woods and actually shot themselves rather than face another fruitless session with their faculty advisor or stare once again into the emptiness of an imagination gone blank.

The system emerges

So there I was, twenty-nine years old, with a wife and a nine-month-old daughter, living in student housing euphemistically called "Victory Village" and made of converted WWII navy barracks. When you put a tack in the wall to hang a picture in one victory village apartment, the point would poke through the wall next door.

I was not interested in Marvin's five years, and solitary, despondent walks in the woods had never appealed to me. So I

While at the University of North Carolina, I stumbled upon a system which enabled me to write my dissertation so effortlessly and so smoothly that I completed it in nine months.

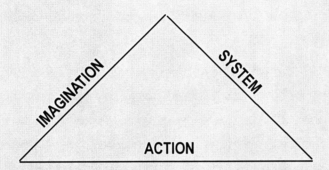

The Creative Triad

IMAGINATION creates the ideas that books are made of. But imagination remains passive without the SYSTEM required to generate and collect your ideas. Both of these rest upon the power of ACTION, which translates your ideas into real pages in real books, in the real world

summoned all my will power and set to work.

I made one false start by choosing to write something about Simone de Beauvoir, the French novelist, diarist and feminist who was long the companion of Jean-Paul Sartre. I just wasn't sure what I wanted to write about her. I had chosen the topic simply because it was there. In those days de Beauvoir was not much known in the United States. I floundered around for quite a while looking for an angle.

I never found one. The truth was that I didn't much like Simone de Beauvoir or her work. I found her stuffy, rigid, and boring. And when I read that Nelson Algren, once her American lover, observed that she had kept her hair in that bun for years, never taking it down even to wash it, I decided that I was through with her.

So I started over, but this time on the right track. One thing I knew for sure: I would choose to write about someone whose work interested me. I settled on the French poet Stéphane Mallarmé. I was enthusiastic about the project and began assembling the information I needed.

So doing, I stumbled upon a system which enabled me to write my dissertation so effortlessly and so smoothly that I completed it in nine months, presenting it to my advisor *en toto*, as a finished product. He liked it, accepted it on behalf of the department, and recommended that I submit it for publication. I did so, and the University of Georgia Press published it: *Mallarmé and the Language of Mysticism*, my first book. I was never intimidated by a blank, Blue Horse notebook again.

Since that time I have used my book writing system over and over, and it has never failed. I have written books of biography, folklore, local history, how-to books for writers and self-publishers, —fourteen books so far, and more coming as fast as I found time to write them.

The best thing about my book writing system is that it is transferable. It will work for anyone who used it. Up to now I've shared it on a one-on-one basis. In this manual, I go public.

The Problem with EBooks

My first publishing company owned one of the old hot-lead linotype machines that was still in use. Rube Goldberg would have ben proud of it. I even wrestled it down and learned to use it myself.

Today I'm still wrestling, but this time with eBooks. The whole idea is intriguing. Writing them is no problem. Producing them is cost-free. But how to promote and sell them?

Nobody seems to know. Here's the situation as it now stands: writers and publishers produce the content. Reading device and software companies are vying to produce eBook reading devices. The trouble is that they are all different, these devices. And this lack of a standard, open-source product delivery system for eBooks is the bottleneck that keeps the system from working. If bookstores required shoppers to purchase special glasses costing hundreds of dollars to read the books on their shelves, and the glasses that worked for one store would not work for another, the whole business of bookselling would be kaput.

Amazon.com has developed an ebook reader that has been well-recieved, but it is expensive and proprietary. Only those books especially formatted for it and sold by Amazon can be read on it.

· 2 ·

Step One: Gathering the Tools

YOU WILL FIND IT HARD to believe at first, but in one short visit to the Office Depot or Staples you can pick up your stash of essential book-writing materials. It will cost you about twenty bucks.

No substitutions, please.

Don't be tempted to use something else, something that you think will work just as well. Buy exactly what I tell you to buy and use it in the way that I describe to you. Steer especially clear of those stiff little index cards that your teachers love so much, even if you have a life-time supply on hand left over from the last time you went out and bought school supplies. They're too bulky, inflexible, hard to handle, unstable if piled too high, and you can't get a paper clip on more than a few of them at a time. Plus, they don't easily fit inside the special folders that you will learn how to make..

The best thing about my book writing system is that it is transfer- able. It works for anyone who uses it.

Here's your what you buy:

1. *Five number two pencils* and some kind of sharpener to keep good points on them. Blunt pencils are depressing

2. *Five ball-point pens* with retractable points. Actually, you only need one, but you will misplace at least four of them during the course of getting your book written.

3. *A half-dozen pocket-sized notebook*s, sturdy enough to carry with you wherever you go and survive the wear and tear of travelling around in your purse or back pocket. The best ones are the little. 3.5 by 6 inch booklets manufactured by Avery-Dennison. These are sewn at the spine and last forever. The least useful are those bound with a metal spiral. The spiral tends to get sprung and catch on your pocket after a week or two of use.

4. *Two reams of office copy machine pap*er. You can buy the expensive, heavier grades if your sense of style demands it, but the three or four dollar a ream varieties work just as well. The heart of my book writing system consists of a stack of a few hundred 5.5 by 8.5 slips of paper, plus some folded over 8.5 by 11 sheets to serve as coverlets to store the smaller slips in. Don't laugh. If you do, you may be making one of the biggest mistakes in the course of the literary career you hope someday to have. No, take me very seriously. When you use and manipulate these little slips and these notebooks exactly as I tell you to, your book will practically write itself. It's not magic, but it's as close to magic as any successful

The system is organic. Every part—even the smallest part— works with all the others to create the result you want: a good, strong, well-written book.

book writing system is likely to get.

5. *Cut paper.* Take your paper over to the duplicating center and ask if they have a paper cutter. Give them about four-fifths of your paper and ask them to cut it in half (into 5.5 by 8.5 pieces). Keep the rest of your paper whole. If they do not have a bulk paper cutter, you can take your stuff to a small print shop and ask them to cut it for you. It will just take a minute. Obviously, you can use a hand-lever type table-top cutter, but these take much longer and are nowhere near as neat. Personally, I like my paper to stack up neatly, with no roughly-trimmed edges sticking out from the stack. I call these 5.5 by 8.5 sheets my "idea slips." More about this later.

6. *Homemade folders.* Now for the whole sheets you've got left over. Take each of them, fold them neatly over in the middle so that they form a kid of folder the same size as your note sheets. These will become your "chapter folders." Keep them handy for use.

These simple items constitute your complete book writing kit. With this kit in hand, you can proceed to step two, freeing up your mind for more important things and collecting the ideas that, whether you know it or not, are *always flowing there.*

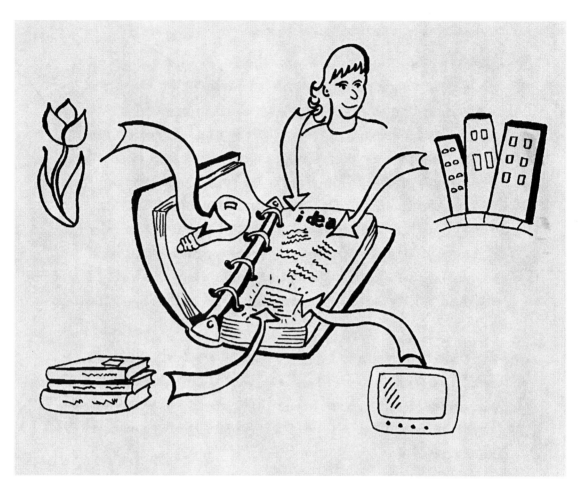

A well thought out Master Idea is a powerful organizing force. It will focus your attention in a way that you may never have experienced before and relentlessly attract usable ideas from every source in your surroundings: nature, the workplace, friends, books, even the tube. It then assimilates them, mingles them with your Master Idea, and makes them your own.

·3·

STEP TWO: DEFINE YOUR MASTER IDEA

THE NEXT, ABSOLUTELY INDISPENSABLE step in getting your book underway is to formulate, clearly and distinctly, the Master Idea that you want to incorporate in it.

The power of a Master Idea

A well-defined Master Idea has immense creative and organizing power.

— It will be your guide to everything you will be writing and thinking in the next few months.

— It will generate ideas on its own, ideas that rise up into consciousness totally unbidden and on their own.

— It will reveal hidden connections between your own ideas and those that you encounter in reading or in conversation.

— It will act as the center point around which your ideas can and will order themselves.

The magnet and the filings

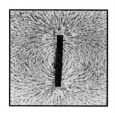

The magnet in this illustration organizes the iron filings that surround it into a co-herent pat-tern, just as your Master Idea organiz-es the random ideas that your mind generates into coherent, usable patterns

Think of the experiment with the magnet and the iron filings that every kid does sometime during his or her public school years. The filings are sprinkled on the top of a piece of illustration board. So sprinkled, they fall randomly, forming no discernible pattern. But when you place a magnet beneath the board on which the filings lie, they suddenly arrange themselves perfectly along the lines of the invisible force exerted by the magnet beneath them.

Your mind—just like my mind and all other minds—is filled with ideas, thoughts, desires, urges. But until you shape them into a pattern they are useless to you. They remain random, like the filings before they encountered the magnetic field. Your Master Idea, like the magnet, pulls your ideas together and makes them available for use. It takes your vague, maybe even fearful, notion of writing a book and turns it into a fully realizable project. Before you define your Master Idea, you just want to write a book. Now you can write it.

John F. Kennedy's Master Idea.

In 1961, President John F. Kennedy formulated one of the most compelling Master Ideas of the century. Addressing a joint session of the congress, Kennedy declared his belief that "this nation

28

should commit itself to achieving the goal, before this decade is out, of landing a man on the moon and returning him safely to the earth. No single space project in this period will be more impressive to mankind, or more important for the long-range exploration of space."

A year later, in a speech at Rice University, Kennedy added that "We choose to go to the moon in this decade . . . because that goal will serve to organize and measure the best of our energies and skills, because that challenge is the one that we are willing to accept, one we are unwilling to postpone. . . ."

A well-developed Master Idea, Kennedy knew, combines two essential ingredients.

1. *It is clear and definite.* We are not going to "do something important in space," or "achieve great things." No, Kennedy said, we are going to send a spacecraft to the moon; it will be a manned spacecraft; and we will do it within "this decade."

2. *It possesses an organizing power* sufficient to achieve the goal that it defines.

Napoleon Hill's take on master ideas.

In the days when I was a college professor, my good friend Bob Stone, a very successful businessman. tried to tell me about the

> Your Master Idea, like the magnet, pulls your ideas together and makes them available for use. It takes your vague, maybe even fearful, notion of writing a book and turns it into a fully realizable project.

"transforming" (his word) ideas of a self-help writer called Napo- leon Hill. At that time I wasn't ready to hear what he was saying. After all, I was an associate professor of comparative literature at a top-ranked college, an academic hot-shot, who, I am the first to admit, looked down my nose at "popular" writers like Hill. Besides, with a name like Napoleon hill, how could he possibly have anything to teach me?

Soon, though, writing unreadable (and unread) "scholarly" articles for the Modern Language Journal began to lose its charm for me, and I decided to see if I could make a living in the real world of writing and publishing instead of merely talking about it in my classroom. I resigned my professorship to own, edit and publish a small weekly newspaper and began working eighteen hours a day at becoming as successful a writer and businessman as Bob Stone was.

Suddenly I began to understand and use what Napoleon Hill had to say. Here's his take on Master Ideas (he calls it "definite- ness of purpose"): *"There is one quality,"* he said, *"that one must possess to win, and that is definiteness of purpose, the knowledge of what one wants, and a burning desire to possess it. The battle is all over except the shouting when one knows what is wanted and has made up his mind to get it."*

Once the Master Idea is formulated, Hill tells his readers, get started immediately on the job of turning it into reality. This is powerful advice: *Do it now! Take immediate action toward the goals you have defined.* Delay is the enemy of action. "Do not wait," Hill said. "The time will never be 'just right.' Start where you stand, and work with whatever tools you may have at your command, and better tools will be found as you go along." Hill understood, as few others have, the effectiveness of Master Ideas in guiding—consciously and unconsciously—our efforts to convert our ideas and goals into real things in the real world, to convert the contents of our minds into books

Mallarmé and me

As I have said, I worked out my book writing system when I was faced with the job of writing a doctoral dissertation. I had decided I wanted to write something on the French poet Stéphane Mallarmé. Still, my intention to write a book about Mallarmé was too general and diffuse to be of any use to me. But just then I happened to read Williams James' book, *The Varieties of Religious Experience*. In it, James listed five characteristics of typical mystical experiences: self-validation; the assurance of the oneness of things; the transitory nature of the experience itself; the life-changing nature of its impact; and the virtual impossibility of communicating to others the essence of the experience itself. It suddenly occurred to me that James' list could be applied to Mallarmé's work in a way that would open his poetry to readers in a new and revealing way.

My Master Idea

This sharpening of my intention converted my vague desire to

> The good news is that you don't have to believe the system will work. Just do the things I tell you to do and you will see for yourself!

A Tip for Writers: Density of Information

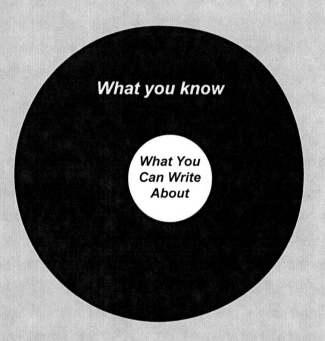

There's another lesson here: Be fully informed about your topic. Clear and distinct ideas imply that you already know a good deal about the subject at hand, whether by personal experience or by reading and research. Good books have a certain density of information, and this density comes from rich personal experience and wide reading in the area of your topic. You can't fake this, although some of us try it from time to time.

"work on" Mallarmé into a powerful Master Idea.

> I decided to write a book called *Mallarmé and the Language of Mysticism*. In this book I would explain Mallarmé's poetry by placing it in the tradition of the writings of western mystics as presented by William James. And I decided to get started immediately.

I realize that few of you, if any, will be interested in writing a book on a foreign poet you've never heard of. But the same things that made this book idea work for me—a well-defined Master Idea and a technique for converting it to well-organized words on a page—will work for any other book project. It will work for yours.

Here's another of my Master Ideas, still awaiting my attention: It is for a book called *An Explorer's Guide to Inner Space*:

> *I am going to write a book about extra-sensory perception and psychical research aimed at the adult reader who is neither scientist nor kook but who has a natural curiosity about the "world beyond the reach of the senses." In it, I will utilize a rich, anecdotal style, collecting a new body of material that does not rely on repetitions of the old stories that readers have heard dozens of times. I will show skeptical but interested readers why they should not only believe that these events occur, but how they themselves can experience them."*

Redfield's Master Idea.

I can imagine James Redfield, author of the *The Celestine Prophecy*, feeling very good after he had formulated this Master Idea:

> *I am going to write a story that will incorporate important insights into the human condition and how to improve it. To do so, I will invent an ancient manuscript, written in Aramaic and suppressed by the organized church, and reveal its lessons one by one to the hero of my story, a seeker who must travel from the US to an exotic location—Peru—in his search for understanding. I will present nine insights in this book and save the tenth and last one as a teaser for a sequel,* The Tenth Insight.

Redfield wrote his book. Redfield is not a great writer, but he defined his idea, collected and organized his thoughts, sat down at his desk, put words on paper and produced a best-seller. Who says Master Ideas don't work?

**Use the space below to take a stab at formulating
your own Master Idea.**

• 4 •

STEP THREE: TAKING OUT THE
(MENTAL) GARBAGE

IS THERE A TRACE of self-doubt lurking in the back of your mind? Do you still think you can't do it? In spite of what I am saying, do you still think that you are going to keep banging your head against the creative wall that has been hemming you in? OK, let's deal with it.

Cleanse your mind of all that hinders it.

First of all, let's get take out the mental garbage, the fear of writing a one hundred, two hundred, or three hundred page book (or more!) can strike into your heart. The good news is that when you use my book-writing system, you don't even have to think about "writing a book"—terrifying words for someone who has not done

"Act as if it were impossible to fail. That is the talisman, the formula, the command of right-about-face which turns us from failure towards success."
- Dorothea Brande

37

it before. Just make one little notebook entry at a time. One idea, One entry. Anyone can do that, so long as you have ideas in the first place. *And everybody has ideas, including you.*

But many—even most—of us discount our own ideas long before they occur to us and, valueless things that they appear to us to be, allow them to simply disappear and vanish into thin air. When we learn to respect our own creative energies and processes and stop discounting them, we have taken the first step toward writing our book.

Mind power

Your mind is a far richer in ideas, far more powerful in refining and developing them, far more capable of great imaginative power than you ever thought possible. That's right, *your* mind. Not my mind, not your best friend's mind, nor even your favorite author's mind. *Your* mind.

"Yeah," you complain, as you face yet another blank page. "But where are these ideas? I haven't noticed any great ones lying around lately."

I sympathize. I've been there and used to say the same thing. Until I was twenty years old and a sophomore in college I didn't know I had any ideas at all. My high school "education" had pretty well beaten all the imagination out of me. Then

Sam discovers he really does have ideas of his own!

38

I found a way to liberate the power of my own mind, and everything changed. Since then, I have helped dozens of others do the same thing, and now I'm helping you. So pay attention. I promise: everything I say in this chapter is tried and true, and *everything I advise you to do will work.*

Accepting our own creativity

Our problem is not so much to become creative as to recognize and accept the creativity that we already possess. Understanding that the human mind—every last one of them, including yours—is a 24-hour-a-day non-stop idea factory is the first, giant step toward the liberation of your book writing potential. That's its nature. That's what it does. Our minds are constantly generating and emitting ideas. When we do not honor our own ideas by paying attention to them, we force them back into the dark recesses from which they emerged, where they lie dormant or simply burn out and disappear. The more we ignore our own creativity, the less accessible it becomes to us. But the reverse is also true. The more attention we pay to our ideas, the more we and the trouble to capture and record them, the more numerous they become.

Your Master Idea is always chugging away in the background while you are doing something else in the foreground of your mind, maybe even something you consider totally unproductive.

So why don't we do this? Here are some of the reasons. Most of us will easily recognize them from our own experience. For most writers they are old, old enemies.

On Self-Criticism

Those of you who are very meticulous about everything you do—perhaps even harboring a certain perfectionism—may be feeling a bit uncomfortable about now. All this freeing up of the imagination is well and good, but when do you start refining what it produces? Immediately? Not on your life. You are tempted to start whittling away at what you have done before you ever finish doing it.

Don't give in to this impulse. There will be plenty of time for that later.

After you get your book on paper—all of it—go back over to edit and polish. You may find that several paragraphs in, say, Chapter Seven really fit better in Chapter Two, and that the illustration in Chapter Three fits better in Chapter Six. And you can check one by one for readability, rhythm, anecdote, transitions, the telling detail, suppleness of style and the handling of quotes—in short for all the things I tell you about in the Chapter Ten of this book.

1. ***We have had the imagination educated out of us.*** Much of our childhood education is spent squeezing the imagination out of us. It prepares us, at best, for the SAT exams that we take as high school seniors to get into college. Unfortunately, these multiple choice obstacle courses only measure the facts we have in our heads. The SAT has a section on verbal skills and a section on mathematical skills. It has no section on creative skills and does not measure what we can imagine. Yet it is the imagination that is the great creative force. It tells us what to do with those facts. It was a fact that steam, like other expanding gasses, exerted pressure on the vessel that contained it. It was imagination that invented the steam engine.

> A young person is truly lucky to have had one single teacher who understood the power and value of the imagination and taught his students about it. And men and women who accomplish things are those who combine a native intelligence with imagination and—the third side of this creative triad—energy. *For writers, that means having brains enough to write in the first place, imagination to figure out what to write about, and the energy to do the actual writing once you are ready.*

2. ***We are our own worst critics.*** With friends like ourselves, who needs enemies? For whatever reason, many of us don't value our own ideas. Yet we are all human beings; we all share the same life experiences; we are all caught up in the mystery of what life is all about. Are there strange beings in outer space? You bet. It's us. We are as strange as they come.

The SAT does not measure imagination, yet it is imagination that is the great creative force.

How could such strange, mysterious, complex beings *not* have a creative imagination?

Respect your own mind. It really is a miracle. Nourish and protect the ideas that it constantly produces. I learned to do this the hard way. There was a time when, whenever I sat down to write, someone else sat down with me, and that somebody was no admirer of mine. Perched on my left shoulder, he would peer over my head to read what I had just written. "You call that writing?" he would say. "Who do you think you are, Shakespeare? Why don't you quit messing with that trash and go sell used cars for a living?"

It was some time before I realized that the guy doing the hatchet job on my work was . . . me. I finally told myself to shut up and began to trust my own ideas. Writing suddenly became far easier. Not that I am incapable of self-criticism. I am. But it is criticism aimed at improving what I have written, not at keeping me from writing anything at all.

> The human mind —every last one of them, including yours—is a 24-hour-a-day, non-stop idea factory.

Bracket it!

It is not that easy to tell the critical part of yourself to shut up. If this is the case for you, here is what you do. Bracket your self-doubts. You can't force them into non-existence, so just make a deal with yourself to ignore them for a while. Admit to yourself that you still question your creative ability, but agree with yourself to set these questions aside, to "bracket" them as something to come back to later. Then go ahead and start using the book-writing system I describe in this book. I promise that when you do return to your brackets, the doubts that once filled them will have disappeared.

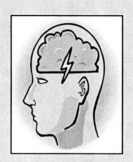

Our Ideas Can Vanish before We Capture Them

Our ideas will disappear on us if we are not careful to capture them. To understand just how evanescent an idea is, imagine this: You are in the wilderness, trying to start a fire with no matches. You strike a piece of flint with a metal bar. Sparks are emitted, but the life of these sparks is the merest fraction of a second. They are gone almost as fast as they appear. But catch one of them in a small pile of tinder, and it will ignite, creating a tiny flame that you can then use to start your campfire, warm your hands, cook your dinner, keep wild animals at bay—whatever you want. Ideas are like those sparks. They come to us when our minds are struck by some event, some conversation or even by some other idea. Like those sparks, they are here one second and gone the next unless we take care to preserve them.

· 5 ·

Step Four: Mind Harvesting

MIND HARVESTING IS THE systematic preservation of the ideas that our minds generate. Ideas not collected as soon as they appear vanish into thin air and are lost forever. Ideas that you collect and develop inevitably reach the critical mass required to create a book.

Earlier, we learned that everything starts with a well-defined idea— a Master Idea—that works like a magnet, attracting to itself all the information, examples, quotes, and anecdotes that you need to flesh out into a book. It is not really magic, but it certainly seems magical.

Like a "multi-tasking" computer that is capable of performing two or more discrete activities simultaneously, the Master Idea is always chugging away in the background while you are doing something else in the foreground of your mind, maybe even some-

homo (The pattern maker)

Most men cannot live without organization — But The function of organize is to eliminate things, to tame or domesticate reality. It hides the nature of the world from us.

Like an air filled float it allows us to hootle safely on The surface

— of life rather than taking the dangerous plunge into its depths —

The "organized" church makes it possible for us to live with religion without being much affected by it

[In The Steps of The Master]

The projection of our wishes and desires put a dose into meaning —

A sample page from one of my pocket notebooks I am now carrying while harvesting ideas for a new book called *Believing and Knowing*. You can see that in quickly jotting down your ideas, neatness does not count. I had just noticed, while thinking about the constellations as we name them, that we compulsively impose patterns on our experience even when patterns are not really there. For a translation of these scribbles, see page 49.

thing you consider totally unproductive. Something like watching "I Love Raymond" or "CSI Miami." Suddenly Raymond, or his Mother, or his Dad—someone—says something or does something that catches your attention on another level. Your Master Idea, always at the ready, has reached out and grasped it. Yes, you say, I can use that in my book. So you take a second or two—that's all it takes—to make sure that the insight you have just had doesn't simply disappear into thin air. Your mind pounces on it, and you pull out one of the pocket notebooks I told you to buy and carry with you at all times, and you jot down your idea immediately and completely.

Your mind pounces on it, and you begin to write. The word "immediately" is an important one here. It means that you don't put off your note-taking for even a second. And here's what I mean by "completely." It often happens that in writing down your thought, related ideas will occur to you. Don't ignore them. Turn a page if necessary and note these down, too.

Don't try to decide what is good and what is bad, what is important and what is not. Just write until you're done. These ideas have come your way because you have a well-defined a Master Idea lying in wait in the back of your mind, ready to seize on any insights that happen by, just as a frog's

Your Master Idea lies in wait like a frog waiting for its next meal.

tongue, lightning fast, flicks out to capture its next meal. Zap, it's done. Another idea in the hopper. Intellectual dinner time.

Once you have captured the essence of the idea-event, put your notebook away and go on with whatever you were doing. When another idea comes along—as it will—drag your notebook out again and record it, too. Continue until your little spasm of creativity has quieted down again and your Master Idea has retired to its lair, in wait for the next idea that comes along.

Take good care of this notebook and the many others that you will surely fill up with your notes. They contain your mind-treasure, the intellectual substance out of which your book will be made. Never discard them. I have often found a later use for ideas preserved in notebooks created earlier for entirely different projects.

This kind of mind-harvesting works the way irrigation does in arid western states. For years no vegetables grew in the parched open lands of Arizona and California. There was rain in the uplands, but it could not be put to work downstream to make land fertile. It was not put to work because the water was not collected in usable quantities. It was flood or famine—or both. But in the first half of the last century great dams were built that slowly impounded this water in vast quantities. Once impounded, the water

Notebook Work

The scribbled notes on page 46 record an idea that occurred to me as I pruned a tree in my backyard to improve its contour. I suddenly realized that the price of my shaping the tree was the destruction of a good part of it. I took out my notebook and wrote the following idea:

"homo (the pattern maker)" Most men cannot live without organization, but the function of organization is to eliminate things, to tame or domesticate reality. It hides the world from me."

Then this elaboration came along: "Like an air-filled float it enables us to bobble on the surface of life rather than take the plunge into its depths."

Then this: The "organized" church makes it possible for us to live with religion without being much affected by it.

Finally: The projection of our needs and desires, not a door into meaning.

These notes were scribbled, as quickly as I could write. I did not worry about grammar, style, completeness. I would look up the Latin for "man the pattern maker" later. Had I not written these ideas down as they occurred they could well have been lost to me forever. All of this took just a minute or two. Then I stuck the notebook in my pocket and went on trimming the tree.

This is my current notebook. It is approximately 3.5 by 5.5 inches in size and sewn at the spine. It is a little the worse for wear but sturdy enough to survive over the long haul. Though you can scarcely read it here, it is marked with the date when I began to use it. I have many such notebooks now, and use them continually.

was distributed to the farms that needed it, when they needed it, and the valleys grew green.

> Your mind—the most richly creative tool in the universe—is constantly giving birth to ideas. Your notebooks, like those dams, impound them and keep them ready for use in your books. Without these intellectual storehouses your ideas simply evaporate. Here today and gone today, too. But with them you irrigate a heretofore unnecessarily arid imagination. Now, all kinds of things will grow there, among them your book.

More notebook samples

Let me give you a few more samples of notebook entries that were very useful to me. Reproduced below are the contents of several more pages from a *Believing and Knowing* notebook. These notes deal with the value of personal religious experience as distinct from passive acceptance of dogma. I transcribe them here word for word. The words in brackets are explanatory and not part of the notebook entry.

I do not remember where I was or what I was doing when these thoughts came to me, but thanks to my notebook, I still have the thoughts themselves. I believe that when you begin to value and store your own insights you will be astonished at the complexity and depth of the ideas that well up from the creative center deep within your mind.

> *The only real problem is the problem of meaning. With meaning all is valuable. Without meaning, nothing is. Examples: Vietnam, Phèdre. Meaning focuses forward. Meaninglessness is utter desolation.* [There is a powerful scene in the first act of Racine's play *Phèdre* in which Phèdre experiences herself and all things around her as stripped bare of all value.]

—*Overcoming the "and yet" syndrome* [This note reminds me to look again at a passage from *Mere Christianity*, by C. S. Lewis on the ease with which the material world can quickly dissipate the most spiritual of insights.]

—*Make friends with the mystery.*

—*The beginning of it all is the "I." But in what kind of world (context) can an "I" exist?*

—*Evelyn Underhill says that "the external world is a work of art, not a scientific fact."* [Underhill's idea prompted the following reflection.] *More faith is needed to accept the perceived world as real than to believe in the reality of the spirit.*

Such notes, as unclear as they may be to anyone else, were sufficient to remind me of what I was thinking at the time. They were born from the mingling of my own Master Idea with whatever I happened to be doing at the time.

My notes were been more practical when I was writing my book on publishing a weekly newspapers. Pages from that notebook contain far more down-to-earth how-to ideas, such as the following:

> *Hitting the wall. Develop the idea that when starting your publication it is not unusual to reach a point where you feel that you simply cannot go further and are tempted to give up. But perseverance and goal-setting enable you to break through and move ahead all the more successfully.*

On another page in the same notebook, I jotted down this idea. I had, as a college professor, grown used to a slim purse. As a publisher, I would be surprised to learn that others had much fatter ones. One day, while calling on an advertising prospect, I realized that I was reluctant to ask for a space order because I felt that I myself could not afford the cost. That was nonsense, and the minute I realized this, my sales calls became much easier and much more successful. So I pulled out my notebook and made this note.

> *Key to ad sales: never judge anyone else's pocketbook by your own. There's more wealth out there than you ever dreamed of, and there*

is no way of knowing who has got it and who hasn't until you ask for the order.

On still another page of this same notebook I noted an idea for a regular feature. I was publishing a weekly newspaper in Davidson, North Carolina, *The Mecklenburg Gazette*. On this day my wife called with the news that there was no hot water coming out of the faucet on our kitchen sink. I was on deadline and could not leave the office. I called my friend Frank Burns, owner of Burns Electric and Plumbing and told him about the problem. He replied, "No problem. I remember when that house was built. I can have it going again in no time." That day Frank Burns was my hero. I realized that Frank had been working in our small town for thirty years, and probably knew more about what was behind every wall in every house that anyone else alive. I decided I would thank him publicly for his work. I then realized that there were many other tradespeople just like him and that they were the glue that held the town together. I pulled out my notebook and made this note:

Feature idea: unsung heroes. Plumbers, electricians, etc. who make the town work but are not usually recognized for their contribution to all our lives. Maybe make this idea into a monthly third editorial.

These ideas eventually found their way out of my notebook and into my book, *Kitchen Table Publisher,* later republished as *Publish Your Own Magazine, Guidebook, or Weekly Newspaper* (Sentient Publications, Boulder, Colorado). This book is now in its sixth edition.

It works for fiction, too

Though we are talking here mostly about non-fiction books, your notebook will work for fiction, too. If I had been working on a novel, my notebooks would have contained not only ideas, but turns of phrase, character-revealing gestures, snippets of conversation, plot complications and resolutions, locales and descriptions.

Ideas on demand?

Could I have gone to my desk and simply willed back into existence the ideas that my notebooks are crammed with? No I could not. I certainly could not have had them all before me at a single moment in time, organized and ready to use. I—and most likely you, too—cannot command my imagination to create. I can't say, "OK, here I am at the keyboard. Feed me the good stuff," although it is sometimes true that if you force yourself to start writing, new ideas will often follow.

Whenever, bidden or unbidden, your imagination decides to produce an idea or insight, it is your job to pay attention and collect these gifts to you from the creative center of your life. They are gifts for sharing, and sharing them is why you are a writer.

Ideas from reading, random and otherwise

We all do a lot of reading, more than we think, probably, and at all levels. There are text books, song books, comic books, mass market novels, genre novels, literary novels, non-fiction books, how-to books, the sports pages, the editorial pages, web pages, sacred books, and the backs of cereal boxes. And everything we read is full of ideas, whether we are reading for simple pleasure, serious instruction or to find out how to do something.

But whenever and for whatever reason we are reading, one thing is sure: sooner or later a thought, observation, trait of character, rhythm or image will sink deeply into us and activate a response from our Master Idea. When this happens, pull out your pencil and make a light notation in the margin of your book, including ancillary thoughts that might have occurred. Then continue reading. I know that we were all trained to think it almost sinful to write in a book or turn down the corner of a page, but pay no attention to those lessons. They came mainly from the textbook commissions that furnished books for public schools. Their job was not to make the books more useful to students but to preserve them for the next thirty kids who would fill up the seats the next year.

If you are using a library book or a textbook that someone else will have to use later, just mark your spot with a light check with

Is it sinful to write in the margins of books you're reading? It may be more sinful not to do so.

a number two pencil. It's that or lose the germ of your idea altogether. You can easily erase these marks later. I prefer to own my own books whenever I can. I can write whatever I want, wherever I want and whenever I want. Picking up a book I read last year, full of marginal notes, annotations and reactions, is like tracing the history of my mind. Such experiences remind me how smart I apparently used to be and cause me to lament the poverty of mind that now seems to have befallen me! Then again, next year I will think the same thing when I open the books I am reading now.

Much of your reading will not be random. It will be done in search of information that will be valuable to you in fleshing out your Master Idea. Your notebook entries taken from any one of these books is likely to contain many more pages than you accumulate from random reading.

Still, follow the same procedure as before. Note the passages that interest you. Then come back to them and think about them. Some you will simply discard; others you will pounce on. The author may have dealt with the same idea later and in a more interesting way. Or you may simply decide that a passage that seemed of interest is not as valuable as you thought it would be. You note down enough of the text to remember it—or the whole passage if you think you might quote from it—and go on to analyze it and add you own observations to it.

•6•

Step Five: Creating Idea Slips

REMEMBER THAT STACK of 5.5 by 8.5 slips you had the printing center cut for you? Get them out. It's time to use them. These "idea slips" will form the backbone of your book.

Transcribing your pocket notebooks

Your pocket notebooks enable you to jot down an idea immediately, whenever or wherever it occurs. However, the notebooks themselves are too random and disorganized to use in your actual writing. You are going to have to get your ideas out of the notebooks and into a form that you can sort and use. Here's how.

> The products of your imagination are gifts for sharing, and the desire to share them is why you are a writer.

   1. Once a week, sit down at your desk with your notebook(s) and your idea slips.

2. Transfer your notes one by one from whatever notebooks you have been working with onto your idea slips—one idea and one idea only per slip.

3. If you already have some idea of where a particular idea will fit into the scheme of your book, note that on the top of the idea slip, then continue with your idea. If the idea comes from a book, note a short title and page number reference at the top.

4. It often happens that as you are transferring your idea to an idea slip, related ideas will pop into your head. Note these down, too. There is room to do so on the larger idea slips. Continue your note onto the back of the slip or even onto a second slip. If you do this, staple the two slips together.

5. Save the transcribed notebooks as your backup and for use in future projects. Store them in a safe place. From this point on you will be working with the idea slips.

6. Put a fresh notebook in your pocket to continue the idea harvest tomorrow, the next day, and all the days after that.

7. You will continue this routine over and over until the time comes for you to sort your idea slips and begin writing.

Marginal notes to idea slips

When you have finished any book you have been reading and in which you have made some marginal notations, take it to your desk and pull out a stack of blank idea slips, then do this:

1. Take one full eight-and-a-half-by-eleven sheet of paper and fold it in half. On the top of the outside page, write the name of the book you are working with, the author, publisher and date of publication. All of such folders, collected later, will make up your bibliographic record.

2. Leaf through your book for any marks you made. Now is the time for making judgements. Simply pass over those that no longer interest you or whose content has been better dealt with elsewhere. When you come upon one that still seems of interest to you, take an idea slip and write the subject matter of your idea on the top. Then write down your idea and perhaps a quote.

Here is an example: I bought a book at a yard sale a week or so ago, *Here at the New Yorker*, by Brenden Gill. I was reading it for pleasure, without any idea that Gill's narrative might contain something that would contribute to the book I was working on, *Believing and Knowing*. Yet on page 166 I came across the following passage:

> *The great abstractions—God, ourselves as an act of special creation, the hereafter—upon which, however indirectly, the fiction of the past was based, have become irrelevant for most of us and, for some of us, simply do not exist. In the lonely*

Buzon, Tony. Using Both Sides of Your Brain. Plume. 1990

This is the front of a folder I made to contain notes and quotes from Tony Buzon's book, *Using Both Sides of Your Brain (see the chapter on unfolding ideas)*. Note that it identifies the author, the title and all the ther bibliographic information I need. now. You can waste a lot of time looking for it later on.

work of writing fiction, we have nothing to fall back on but our self-awareness; understandably we turn from that dark cave, peopled by who knows what attendant horrors, to enter the busily humming, boringly lighted world of concrete and specific facts, where at every turn we are sure to encounter some situation capable of being measured and described and therefore suitable to our needs and accommodatable to our craft. "The odds are with the objects." Maxwell said; he might have added, "And on facts."

I happened to be reading this on the beach, in front of my daughter's home in Fort Lauderdale. Bathing suits are short on pockets, so, against all my own rules and admonitions, I had left my pencil and notebook up at the house. I turned over a corner of the page so that I could find my way back to this passage.

Later that day, back up at the house again, I got out my sheaf of blank idea slips. I doubled a full-sized sheet of in half, forming a 5.5 by 8.5 inch folder. On the top of the front cover of the folder I carefully noted the essential bibliographic information: Gill, Brendan. *Here at the New Yorker,* Random House, 1975. I would put this and any other idea slips generated by Brendan Gill's book into Gill's folder.

Next, I took out an idea slip. At the top I noted Gill, *Here at the New Yorker*, p. 166. Below, I copied the passage that had caught my attention. I tucked this inside the folder I had made and added it to the stack of notes already on my desk. Now it was preserved,

> Mind Mapping 96
>
> "The idea is to recall everything your mind throws up around the central idea. As your mind will generate ideas faster than you can write, there should be almost no pause – if you do pause you will probably notice your pen or pencil dithering over the page. The moment you notice this get it back down and ~~hurry on~~ carry on. Do not worry about order or organization as this will in many cases take care of itself. If it does not, a final ordering can be completed at the end of the exercise."

This is an idea slip I used in writing the "unfolding" chapter in this book. It consists of a quote from page 96 of Tony Buzon's book. The top line identifies book, author topic, and page number.

secure. Whenever I got around to writing on this topic in my book, it would be available to me and, if I so chose, I could cite Brendan Gill's observation to illustrate my own theme.

The other books you read, whether in the same field as yours or in a closely related one, will spark all kinds of creative activity in your mind. They are part of your basic research and the heart of your bibliography. Still, you do not read these books to borrow from them, but to be stimulated by them. Some of the most valuable of my note slips resulted not from an ideas I found fully formed in someone else's book, but from my reaction to those ideas.

Here's an example. When I was working on my book on Mallarmé, I read the book that a critic named Albert Thibaudet had written about the poet. In it I checked an observation that interested me. I later went back to it and entered both the idea and my development of it on one of my idea slips:

Thibaudet, page 48

Thibaudet notes in Mallarmé a fascination with every-day objects and a tendency to deform them into living presences.

I would observe that Mallarmé works a transformation but not necessarily a deformation. And the transformation accomplished is not of the object itself but of the quality of consciousness with which it is apprehended. The transformation of consciousness then does not deform the object but, absolutely open to being (as Heidegger might say) allows it to be what it essentially is, an upsurge into experience of absolute being, offering itself mutely for our contemplation.

Now this may be gobledegook to you—undoubtedly it is—but for me, at the time, it was pure gold and became an important part of my book, *Mallarmé and the Language of Mysticism.*

Don't let the fact that my subject and interests are different from yours put you off. My system will work for any book. Let's say that you are writing a family history, or a book on how to overhaul the engine of a '48 Studebaker, or a guide to writing the perfect business plan, or a book on how to start a home-based business. Such books, when they are really good, are full of anecdotes, illustrations, case histories, insider tips, sidebars, forms, and more. You will get ideas for such books as these from the same sources as I have described in my system: from walking around and talking to whomever you meet; from asking questions; from random reading; from reading the newspaper; from surfing the net; from targeted reading of other books in the field; and everywhere else that you can think of. And you will collect and utilize them in the way I have described.

Your notebooks and idea slips will be filled with the material you need to write knowledgeably about all these topics and many more, preserving the success stories, anecdotes, telling details and other concrete information you need to illustrate your ideas and make them come alive.

· 7 ·

STEP SIX: SORTING THE IDEA SLIPS

AFTER A TIME YOU will have accumulated a sizeable bundle of idea slips and decide that it is time to get started writing your book. These idea slips contain the products of your own creative mind and nobody else's. They are on the desk before you, but they are still not organized in a usable way. So the next step is to sort your idea slips for easy use. Here's how it's done:

1. Find a large work surface, such as dining room table. Take a stack of full-size, 8.5 by 11 sheets of paper. Double them over to make a 5.5 by 8 inch folders. With a Sharpie or similar bold marker, label the front of a folder for each chapter or subject matter area of you book, as determined by your Master Idea. Here's an example. In the last chapter I recorded a Master Idea for a book on starting a home-based business. If I were sorting idea slips for such a book, I might label the category sheets as follows:

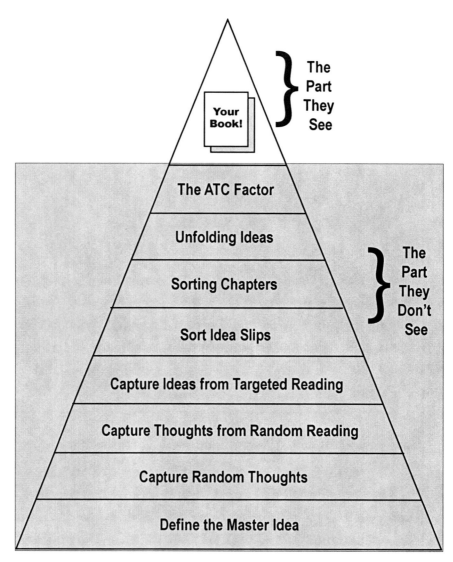

The Writing System Pyramid

- Introduction.

- Getting started.

- Evaluating your idea.

- Start-up costs.

- Projecting profit and loss.

- Secondary profit centers.

- Equipment needed and where to get it.

- Selling your products or service.

- Licenses and fees.

And so on. For my most recent book, *Get Paid to Write*, the chapter folders read as follows

- Introduction.

- Freelancer's tool kit.

- How to write a query.

- Knowing what editors want.

- Getting ideas.

- Secrets of the freelance masters.

- Syndicating a newspaper column.

- Internet opportunities.

- Business writing.

- Structure of an article.

- Contacts and sources.

I made another folder, labeled "other stuff" for ideas that did not find an immediate home but that I would review and fit in later.

2. Once you have your chapter folders done, spread them out, fan-like, on the table top so that the label on the top of each folder is easily visible. Save a little space on the table top for additional folders, since it is unlikely that you will make all you need the first time around.

3. Now take your stack of ideas slips and, one by one, place them on top of the chapter folder to which each, by its nature, belongs. If in doubt, that's OK, too. You will have time to remedy any initial errors later. When you complete this task you will have a dozen or so piles of idea slips, sorted by subject matter. Pick up each pile of sorted idea slips and insert them into their chapter folder and set them aside.

4. Now organize the chapter folders according to the order in which you intend to deal with the subject matter as you write your book.

This stack of folders constitutes the backbone of your book, the vertebral column through which the Master Idea infuses the parts of your book and brings them all together into one organic whole.

Now take the folder labeled "Introduction," and look through it. Sort the slips you find there in the order that makes most sense to you.

This order is tentative. As you write you may decide to adjust it. The act of writing itself will shed light on the ideas you have accumulated and help reveal the logical order that binds them together. Do the same thing with your other folders.

You don't really have to start with the first chapter. You may have been thinking of the subject matter of a later chapter and be geared up to get started on it. Personally, I always begin at the beginning because it helps me understand where I am going. After I've done that, I take up the other chapters as the spirit (and interests of the moment) move me.

At this point you may, as I often do, pick up an idea slip, read it and think, "You know, there's much more to this idea. I've got to expand it a bit."

The following chapter will tell you precisely how you to do that by unfolding your idea and releasing all the content compressed within it. There may be far more of this condensed meaning than you ever thought possible.

Would you mind repeating that? I need it for my book.

· 8 ·

Step Seven: Unfolding Your Ideas

SO YOU LOOK AT the sheaf of notes labeled, say, "Chapter One." How many note slips are in there, fifteen or twenty? Thirty? How, you wonder, are you going to make a chapter out of that? In the form in which you have noted them down, they may amount to two or three hundred words, at most. Yet, what you have before you in that miraculous stack of note slips is the essence of your lead chapter. In meat and potatoes terms, what you've got is the U.S. prime, Black Angus steak. But as good as it is, that slab of fine, red meat is not be enough to make a complete meal. You're still lacking the mashed potatoes and salad, the green beans, corn bread, and strawberry shortcake.

Tom's black hole theory of mind

So where is the rest of your chapter coming from? Let me introduce you to my "black hole theory of mind." This theory grew out of many years of teaching writing in colleges and in writer's workshops and conferences and from many sleepless nights peering into my own mind.

When astronomers look at the sky they see stars everywhere, from horizon to horizon. Except, they point out, for an occasional "black hole" where, apparently, nothing exists at all.

As it turns out, though it looks as though nothing is there, a black hole is not a hole at all. In reality it is the one thing in the universe that is farthest from being empty. It is the densest, most jam-packed space of all. It is so dense and the internal force of its gravity is so great that nothing—*not even light*—can escape from it. *Nevertheless, when a black hole becomes so super-charged with matter that it does explode, the power it releases is akin to the power of creation itself.*

Like these celestial black holes, our minds have their own dark, inaccessible places, into which we unconsciously stuff a great part of our creative imagination. What we need is a creative explosion.

The oak is in the acorn

Our minds—all of them—are dense with ideas, but all this stuff is tightly crammed down in there, like an oak tree crammed down into an acorn. When we survey ourselves and our capabilities, we aren't even aware that the ideas are there. Where we are accustomed to seeing, and accepting, acorns, we've got to see potential oak trees.

I listed earlier the kinds of experience that cause us to cram the imaginative part of us down into that hole in the first place: parents who do not understand the value of self-expression; a teacher who somehow kills rather than nurtures the joy of intellectual exploration; peers who laugh at our early efforts; and that harshest pressure of all, the implacable force of the self-criticism that we level against our own achievements.

We admire the ideas of others but treat our own as though they were of little or no worth. So we've go to do two things:

1. On a theoretical level, we've got to accept the fact that the idea-laden black hole—and therefore our ability to flesh out our ideas so that what appeared to be a single thought becomes a page and a page becomes a chapter—really exists.
2. On a practical level, find a way to decompress the contents of our idea slips so that you can have full access to them in all of their ramifications: every branch and every leaf.

Unfolding the meaning

You don't have to add anything to the idea on your note slip. You just have to give it what it needs to grow, then watch it develop before your very eyes, like one of those tiny, dehydrated sponges that expand to fill your hand once you add a spoonful or two of water.

Mind-mapping

A technique called mind-mapping will do for your ideas what the water does for that sponge. At one of my seminars I met the father of a thirteen-year-old girl who, inspired by Tony Buzan, author of *Use Both Sides of Your Brain*, wrote a little book called *Mind-Mapping for Kids*, which she packaged as a method for getting and developing term-paper ideas when you don't think you have any. It was a simple little book, illustrated with the author's own hand-drawn images. Yet it was so effective that she quickly sold 10,000 copies in the United States and Australia.

There are skeptics who dismiss mind-mapping as a simplistic tool suitable only for amateurs. They are wrong. I have used the technique as a powerful idea generator for many years. Many ideas and even whole sections of this book were mind-mapped before I wrote them

The mind-mapping technique is based on the fact that though we claim to think abstractly we really use free association and images to develop our ideas. We draw pictures in our minds and then think about those pictures. Alfred Einstein began his most revolutionary theorizing by creating what he called "word pictures" to fix his problem before his eyes. Similarly, when we mind-map, we convert abstract thoughts to something we can actually see, drawn out on a page.

Mind-mapping is the intellectual equivalent of a nuclear chain reaction.

How it's done

Mind-mapping (it could just as easily be called idea-mapping) is easy to do, though you have to do it right. It works through idea association and is done almost automatically. Your critical intelligence—the part of the brain that likes to sit around telling you how dumb you are—is put on hold.

Here's what you do:

1. Sit down at a table with a legal pad and a sharp pencil.

2. In the middle of the page, write the word or phrase that identifies the idea that you want to expand.

3. Relax. Let your mind roam free. When a related idea occurs to you, draw a line from the original circle to another word that suggests the new idea. When another idea occurs to you, draw a line

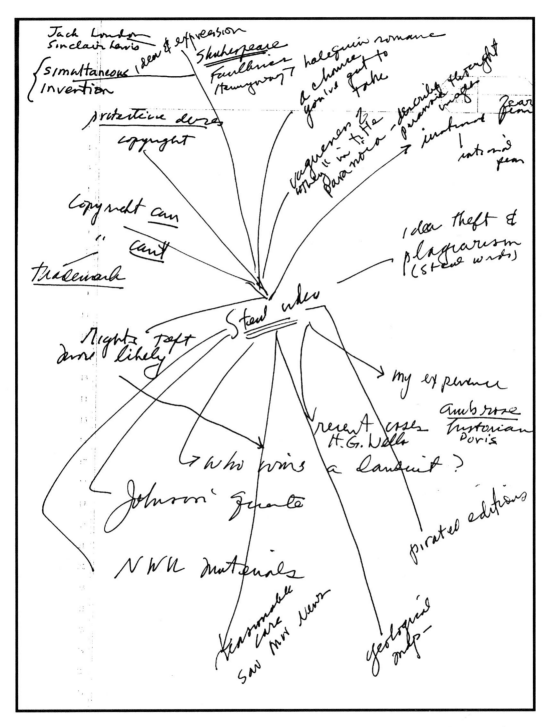

I made this mind map in preparation for writing the chapter "Will They Steal Your Idea" for my book *Get Paid to Write!*

from the main word or the secondary word and to a new word, in which you express a new idea. Sometimes there will be lines from secondary circles to third level circles and beyond.

4. Continue in this way as fast as you can. Don't evaluate as you go. Don't stop to think. Don't draw perfect circles. Don't check spelling. Neatness does not count. Don't worry about drawing straight lines. Just draw.

A mind map even *looks* like an exploding star, radiating meaning from a densely compressed center.

Sound simple? It is, but it works. It is so simple, in fact, that some teachers introduce the technique to students in the middle school years, some even earlier. It is simple that some of my friends, also writers, look askance at it as though anything that a child can use is just not appropriate for an adult, hard-nosed, professional writer.

But they are wrong. Nothing—absolutely nothing—will work as quickly and as well as mind-mapping to expand the super-concentrated, germinal idea that you have written down on the idea slip lying in front of you. Mind-mapping is the intellectual equivalent of a nuclear chain reaction, taking the atom of your idea apart and releasing all the energy compressed within it, or, as in my earlier image, letting the oak tree out of the acorn.

Is this an extravagant claim? It is certainly a strong one, but it is not extravagant. What can I say? It works! It will work the first time you try it, and it will work every time you try it thereafter. I have used the mind-map over and over again, and it has never let me down.

On page 75 I have reproduced the actual mind-map I used to develop ideas for the chapter called "Will They Steal Your Idea," in my book *Get Paid to Write* (Sentient Publications). I scratched it out on a legal-sized, yellow pad.

I wrote as fast as I could, with no self-critical brakes on my imagination. What you see looks pretty much like a scribble. My handwriting is not the clearest in the world even when I am trying, so here is a little help with the deciphering. In the center of the page are the words, "steal idea." This is the idea that I am unfolding, the fear of some beginning writers that others will take what they have written and use it themselves.

Lines extend form the center to clusters of ideas that I jotted down as fast as they popped into my mind. In the upper left hand corner are the names Jack London and Sinclair Lewis. Lewis used to buy short story ideas from London. I thought that this might be a useful example. (As it happens, I didn't use it.) A short line to the right ends with words "idea theft" and "plagiarism (steal words)," reminding me to distinguish between the two. At the top of the page, just right of London's name are the words "idea and expression." And then to the right of that "Shakespeare."

With these words I am reminding myself that there is scarcely anything new or original in the plot of Romeo and Juliet, for instance, nothing not found in many a Harlequin romance. It is the expression of the idea that counts. In the center, left , of the age is the note that "rights theft is more likely" than outright theft of your writing. And so on. By the time I had finished this mind-map, I had topics for the entire chapter spread out before me, not only on my original idea slips, but on additional slips that came from the unfolding of the sometimes compacted ideas on the original slips. All I had to do then was to transfer them to new idea slips and integrate them with the notes that I already had.

Lets sum it up so far:

Step 1. You gathered your materials

Step 2. You defined you master theme

Step 3. You took out the mental garbage

Step 4. You collected the ideas you need to write about it.

Step 5. You preserved these ideas on in your notebooks and on your idea slips.

Step 6. You sorted your ideas into sub-sections or chapters.

Step 7. You used the mind mapping technique to expand any ideas that were unduly compressed.

· 9 ·

THE HORSE'S MOUTH

THERE IS SPECIAL source of unique, very valuable material for your book: the horse's mouth. The horses whose mouths are of most interest to you are those of the leading authorities in your field. Out of those mouths will come expert comments, opinions, observations and evaluations spoken to you and to no one else. Such comments are as precious to you as gold and lend prestige and credibility to your own ideas. If I were writing a book, say, on the legend of Atlantis—and if I could contact anyone I wanted to, living or dead—I would contact Plato himself, who started it all. "Professor Plato," I would say, "I have read everything you have written. You might be surprised to learn that it is not *The Republic* that gets most comment these days, or even *The Symposium*. It is the story of rise and fall of Atlantis. Did you really get that story from your friend Critias, who claims he got it from Salon, who reportedly got it from an Egyptian priest? Or did you just plain make it up yourself?"

And after Plato emailed me back later that afternoon I would be

Writing on Atlantis? Contact Plato.

able to reveal in my book that "Plato himself recently confirmed to me that it was not Salon who first broke the story of Atlantis but an extra-terrestrial he contacted at the Oracle of Apollo, on Mount Parnassus. He explained that he made up the Salon story so people would not think he was crazy."

A quote like that would make news.

Well, you are not writing on Atlantis, and you can't get in touch with Plato. But if you are writing, for instance, on paying the price for political courage, you could contact one or two of the most recent whistle blowers who have lost their jobs by bucking the Washington bureaucracy. If you are writing on gambling and sports, you might try to contact Michael Vick, Pete Rose, any number of NBA referees, or the commissioner of gaming in Nevada. The commissioner of gaming is possible, though you will have the usual front office personnel to get past. But Vick and Rose will be more difficult to reach since, in addition to being—however reluctantly—experts in sports gambling, they are also celebrities. Fortunately, the top people in a given field are often far from stardom and even answer their own phones and read their own mail from time to time. Some years ago, in getting notes together for an article on extrasensory perception, I decided to go straight to the top and get in touch with Dr. J.B. Rhine, head of the Parapsychology Institute at Duke University, the man who transformed the study of telepathy and psychokinesis into a laboratory science. I wrote him as follows:

Dear Dr. Rhine;

I am currently writing a book on the present state of studies in the field of parapsychology. I have carefully studied your ground break-ing books Extra Sensory Perception *and* Extra Sensory Percep-

tion after Sixty Years. I wonder what, from your point of view, the future of the science of parapsychology holds? What directions will research take? What are the most important questions that will be asked and answered?

I would grateful if you could take the time to jot down your response to these questions. For your convenience [This was before the advent of email] *I have enclosed a self-addressed, stamped envelope . . .*

A final paragraph listed my credentials to reassure him of my *bona fides*. I wrote a similar letter to other researchers. Dr. Rhine answered with a personal letter that I still have in my files. So far as I know it contains information that no other writer has.

Another example. Say you are writing a book on making low budget documentary movies. In that book are some nifty, new ideas that you have just come up with. It would be great to quote Michael Moore and Ken Burns. However, since these two these two have attained celebrity as well as expert status, you will be confronted with a veritable jungle of obstacles and flack catchers that may be hard to hack your way through. Make a stab at these luminaries, but quickly turn to others—Chad Hurley and Steve Chen, for instance, the founders of YouTube—who know what they are talking about but who, as non-celebrities, may be more accessible.

Experts by way of experience

An expert is not always the guy from out of town, with three degrees behind his or her name. Some are closer at hand. For instnce, that interests

> A blurb and its author can help provide context or set expectations for an otherwise unknown work and, considered judiciously, may open new doors.
> —Robin Vidimos, The Denver Post

me is the regeneration of blighted neighborhoods. If I were going to write on this subject I would find ground-zero experts to talk to: single mothers, jobless dads, working dads who tough it out and somehow manage to put bread on the family table; politicos who foster civic regeneration and those who hinder it; the oldest person in the neighborhood and the youngest; and business people who manage to survive in blighted areas in spite of the odds.

Find the people who did it, are doing it, or will do it. These you can find wherever you are living. If you are writing about violent streets, remember that the victim of a stabbing is apt to have more authoritative knowledge of that particular crime—and stronger opinions about it—than the university sociologist who has reduced all such cases to a statistic.

But make it your business to get to that sociologist, too, and other national authorities on the subject. Track down Magic Johnson. See how the views of such high-profile individuals mesh with what your prior research has shown you to be the brute, ground-level facts of the case.

Why would experts agree to help you out? Many of them are simply good people who enjoy giving others a hand in a worthy cause. They themselves remember asking for help earlier in their careers and are glad to give it now. Though you may find a curmudgeon or two lurking among them, most are simply people who enjoy talking to other knowledgeable persons about the things that interest them.

Being human, they are also flattered when someone recognizes them for the work they have done and makes it possible for them to show off a bit. And they especially like to talk about what interests them with another person who understands what they have to say and who will, in turn, quote them in such a way as to further enhance their expert status. This is especially true for professors, who save up and count such instances to give them leverage for promotions, raises and the granting of tenure.

Step by step, here's how to organize your search for expert quotes and endorsements.

1. *First, get the names.* If you have been working in a given field long enough to write a book about it, you will already be familiar with the names of the leading authorities in it. Write these down to start your list. In addition, read through magazines and other publications for articles on your subject. Add the names of the authors of these articles to your list. Check the *Reader's Guide to Periodical Literature* for additional names. Review the "find expert" sites on the internet.

2. *Second, gather street and email addresses and telephone numbers*: Here you can face—though not always—a bit of a problem. Sometimes you will find yourself in the position of a salesman who has to thread his way through a phalanx of receptionists, assistants and executive secretaries to finally reach the person to whom you have to sell your product. In such cases look for a personal email account or a home address or telephone number.

In trying to get endorsements for my book *We Choose America,* I wanted to get a copy into the hands of W. Clement Stone, the insurance magnate and author of the classic *Success Through a Positive Mental Attitude.* I located a number of business addresses for Mr. Stone, but kept looking. In *Who's Who in America* I found a home address and sent my advance copy there. Three weeks later

Experts are often easy to talk to and wish to help out in any way they can.

I received a congratulatory letter, the endorsement I sought, and an invitation to send my book to a publishing house in which he had an interest to achieve wider circulation. There are many of these "Who's Who" type directories available to you, regional, national and professional. If your expert is an academic, check faculty directories. Check city telephone directories. Do a Google search and track down every link. Keep looking until you nail down the email, street address, or telephone number most likely to result in personal contact.

3. *Make your approach.* There are three ways to approach your expert: email, telephone and snail mail. Whichever you choose, be direct, brief and to the point. Let your target expert know, first of all, that you are familiar with and admire his work. Then tell him what your project is and why his ideas are important to you. Finally, tell him precisely how he can help you out. Follow this with a word or two about your own credentials.

This in essentially the formula I used in my letter to J.B. Rhine. Today, I would send an email, which is faster and easier. You want to make it as easy as possible for your source to respond, and an email response is swift and effortless. What's easier than to click on the reply button and write a brief note in response to your query? Send enough of these emails and letters out and you will get some replies that will be useful both in writing and in promoting your book.

A telephone call is at the bottom of my list. From the git-go you are battling against the "what's this guy selling" syndrome, but if you can get past this obstacle, the telephone can work very well.

Snail mail requires the most effort on the part of your expert. Your letter must be opened—hopefully by the person it was intended for and not a secretary—read, and replied to. Then the reply must be stuffed in your SASE and put into the "out" box for mailing. That's a lot of steps to have to take in this electronic age.

4. *Always set the stage for follow up.* If you have to call back to verify a fact or check a quote you don't want your expert thinking, "What's this guy want now? Is he going to be a pest" To avoid this, always ask if you can call back to "make sure I get this right." That way your follow up will not be an annoyance but welcomed as a sign of your professionalism.

5. Always send a note of thanks and, when your book appears, a signed copy of it.

The First Five Pages

Professional editors, literary agents, and even browsers in bookstores don't have time to read scores of pages to decide whether they are interested or not in what you have to say. At most they will read the first few pages and, if they find something of interest there, scan through the rest of the book rapidly, checking for your ability to use the language without committing too many of the beginner's mistakes described in the next chapter. They do this because they are also looking for a reason to throw your book aside and go on to the next one.

If you want others to read your book, the first paragraph, then the first four or five pages are the key. Be sure the reader is hooked early on and drawn into the heart of what you have to tell him. The job of the first paragraph is to make the reader want to read the second paragraph—and so on right through the book. Make sure that you have carefully rewritten and revised your work to eliminate every possible stylistic snag.

· 10 ·

THE WRITING ITSELF: TIPS FROM AN OLD PRO'S TOOLKIT

I HAVE TAKEN YOU through a seven-step system that will enable any literate person to write a book. In this chapter I will tell you some of the things you need to know if you want to write a *good* book, one that readers easily read, understand and enjoy. Finally, I will share with you the absolute importance of the widely-known but seldom observed ATC factor. If you don't know what ATC is, I'll make it clear later.

Little things make big differences

The runner who is a tenth of a second faster in the hundred yard dash goes to the Olympics. The runner who is a tenth of a second slower stays home. An average temperature rise of two degrees a year can melt a glacier or change the vegetation of a continent.

The writer who studies and masters the few basic professional writing skills that follow, produces books and articles that are publishable. The one who ignores them does not.

The ten-second sort

An editor to whom you have submitted your work and a bookstore browser who has picked your book up off the rack are both looking for two, but contradictory, things:

1. A reason to keep on reading

2. A reason to put your book down and pick up someone else's.

Yes, this guy really IS a better writer than you are. But don't let that stop you. He's better than everyone else, too.

The bookstore has thousands of books on the shelf, but the usual browser is only going to buy one or two of them. He glances at the cover, turns the book over to read the information on the back cover, and opens it to scan a paragraph or two. This takes no more than ten seconds.

The editor, too, picks up your manuscript hoping that it will be his next best seller. But he will not keep hoping long if you do not give him reason to do so. He gets hundreds of manuscripts a month to look at, and his time is very precious. So, while he is also hoping for the big score, he is also looking for a reason to discard an unsatisfactory submission as quickly as possible. This takes about ten seconds.

What makes a book good or bad on such a cursory examination? The bookstore browser may not be fully aware of the reasons for his reactions, good or bad, though he has them all the same. You can be sure that an editor is very much aware of his. The following is list of things sure to turn editors off. I know, because I read submissions all the time

**Two Iron-Clad Rules for Writers
(Courtesy of Dorothea Brande)**

Iron-Clad Rule Number One:
You cannot create and criticize simultaneously.

Iron-Clad Rule Number Two:
Act as though it were impossible to fail.

A critical faculty is a good thing. We all review and edit, polish and shape what we write. But everything in its time and place. When you hear that little voice whisper in your ear, "You call this slop writing? Why don't you take up podiatry?" — when you hear this voice, snap back at it, "I'll get to you later, Buster. Right now leave me alone!

We are all tormented by this self-critical faculty, and the better we get the more we suffer from it. Creativity is like the water in your garden hose: when you're out watering the daisies and getting only a dribble from the nozzle, you can bet that there's a kink somewhere. Shake the kink out and the water flows freely. The little voice that beats up on your ego is just that: a kink in the hose. Put it in its place: "I'll get to you later, Buster. Right now, shut up. I am busy writing."

for my own press, Williams & Company, Book Publishers, and glanced at thousands of free-lance article submissions when I was publishing my magazines.

1. Inappropriate or inconsistent tone.

It is a little hard to define *tone*, but everyone knows what it is. You could say, for instance, that tone is the flavor of a magazine: comic/humorous (The Onion); yuppie (Gentlemen's Quarterly); scientific/abstract (Scientific American); down home (Mother Earth News); sophisticated (New Yorker); nothing-but-business (Wall Street Journal); highbrow, (Atlantic Monthly).

Subject matter may require a certain tone. The tone of your writing may be appropriate for one topic but not for another. Whatever the requirements of tone are in a particular case, you must zero in on it and maintain it throughout your work .

2. Omission of the telling detail.

The telling detail gives density and believability to any article and helps maintain focus and tone. Compare these two sentences:

"I walked up the stairs and knocked at the door"

"I hurried up the stairs and knocked at the sagging door that someone had recently painted it a sad, pale gray. Small bristles from a cheap brush were still embedded in the crust of the finish."

The first version is inert: generic stairs and generic door, communicating nothing at all. The second gives details that characterize the entire ambiance of the action.

You don't need much, just a stroke here and a stroke there. In this way you incorporate the little things that introduce personality and truth into your writing. Without the wrinkled trench coat and last-legs Peugeot convertible, the character we are watching on TV would be just another detective. With them we are watching a richly-characterized investigator named Columbo. The details do the trick.

The lesson here: Look for and communicate the telling detail, and in doing so always prefer the specific word to the abstract or general word.

3. Awkward handling of dialogue.

Quotes and dialogue—the lifeblood of both non-fiction and fiction writing—are very often clumsily used by some writers. When it comes time to insert a quote inexperienced writers seem to panic and get the dirty work done any way they can.

A dead giveaway of quote-handling trouble is the use of the words "states" or "stated" as substitutes for "says" or "said." I can't explain the fondness of some writers for this stilted phrasing, but when I meet it early on in a piece, I know that I am reading the work of a writer who hasn't mastered his craft. This is usually just the tip of the iceberg. I am not surprised to find other traces of amateur status as I read on. If I read on.

In general, people do not "state" things, they "say" things. How many times have you said something like, "I saw Tom yesterday, and

Vigorous writing is concise. A sentence should contain no unnecessary words, a paragraph no unnecessary sentences, for the same reason that a drawing should have no unnecessary lines and a machine no unnecessary parts. This requires not that the writer make all his sentences short, or that he avoid all detail and treat his subjects only in outline, but that every word tell.
—William Strunk and E. B. White, *The Elements of Style*

he stated that he was going on vacation." I'll wager that you have never said it. What you do say is that you saw Tom and he said that he was going on vacation. In a police report, people state things, and when the President asserts this or that to be true, he may state things. But ordinarily we simply say things.

So we will avoid the "stated" trap at all costs. We will also vary the way we structure our quotes. There are basic three ways to introduce them into your narrative: via the up-front "said," the tail end "said," and "said" in the middle.

Take the sentence: "Tarzan said, 'My best friend is a hairy ape.'" In this example, the "said" is up front.

In the sentence, "My best friend is a hairy ape," said Tarzan, the "said" is of the tail end variety.

But one can also say: "My best friend," said Tarzan, "is a hairy ape." This is the "said in the middle" version. And that's just for starters.

Another technique that allows for characterization is the use of other verbs than "said" to give more specific meaning to the general word. "My best friend," Tarzan bragged, coming to a sudden realization of his good fortune, "is a hairy ape." You can also substitute another, more descriptive, word for "said." "My best friend," smiled Tarzan, "is a hairy ape," or "My best friend," Tarzan lamented, "is a hairy ape, and an ugly one at that."

4. Clumsy transitions.

Transitions relate the parts of your writing to one another in a logical and orderly way. Like the joints of our bodies—and every bit as important—transitions propel the reader along the path you want him to take.

With strong transitions, your writing becomes a functioning, organic whole, delightful to read and easy to understand. Without them, your article consists of disjointed clumps of written matter, which, at best, drag themselves painfully along from beginning to middle to end—if any reader is willing to stick with you that far.

The word "also," stuck alone at the beginning of a paragraph is a common symptom of transition trouble. It is usually stuck there doing duty for some other word that ought to be there but is not. Like the word "stated," the up-front "also" is a dead giveaway that the writer who put it there has not learned how to use transitions.

The job of transitions is to relate each paragraph or thought to the next one in a logical, immediately understandable way—explicit or implied. Explicit transitions consist of words and phrases like *in addition, moreover, therefore, for example, meanwhile, on the other hand, in the last analysis,* and a great many others. Though the meanings of some of these words are similar, they are not interchangeable. Think carefully and write carefully when choosing one of them.

Other transitions are less explicit. The lead sentence of a paragraph can indicate in a number of ways its relation to the paragraph that preceded it and serve as transition. In one of my books about the publishing business, I wrote this paragraph:

"One of the great problems in publishing a weekly newspaper is the scheduling of time. Ad sales, editorial deadlines, layout, printing—all this has to be done on time, day after day, week after week. You can't let anything slip and still get out a newspaper on time.

I began the next paragraph this way: "When I was editor of the Mecklenburg Gazette, I . . . . "And I go on to tell how I encountered and overcame the problem of schedule slippage. "When I was editor of the Mecklenburg Gazette" is the transitional phrase that lets the reader know that an example illustrating the previous statement is coming his way. With this transitional sentence in place, the more explicit "for example" is not necessary.

Other transitions.

I will mention two additional, widely-used techniques for creating transitions.

The first is that of the transitional question. In the above example on newspaper scheduling, my second paragraph might have begun, "How did I handle it?" using a question to direct the reader's attention toward the point I wanted him to absorb. You will see the question/transition often, even though it is not as elegant as some other techniques.

A second transitional technique, and one favored by some editors, is the use of subheads within the text of the article. Subheads lead the reader along, focussing his attention. Subheads also serve to break solid columns of text in a way that makes them seem less daunting and more readable.

Whichever technique you choose, the transition must be there, and it must work.

5. Lack of anecdote and example: the freelancer's paradigm

For many years I published regional magazines and weekly newspapers. To help beginning writers whip their material into shape for these traditional "break-in" markets, I explained to them that anecdote and personal

A Master Speaks

"I had written three other novels before Carrie—*Rage, The Long Walk*, and *The Running Man* were later published. *Rage* is the most troubling of them. *The Long Walk* may be the best of them. But none of them taught me the things I learned from Carrie White. The most important is that the writer's original perception of a character or characters may be as erroneous as the reader's. Running a close second was the realization that stopping a piece of work just because it's hard, either emotionally or imaginatively, is a bad idea. Sometimes you have to go on when you don't feel like it, and sometimes you're doing good work when it feels like all you are managing is to shovel shit from a sitting position."

—Stephen King, *On Writing*

experiences were the lifeblood of readable articles. In doing this, I put the structure basic to all good nonfiction writing into "one-two-three" form and gave it a name: the "freelancer's paradigm."

Results were immediate when writers adopted he paradigm. Marginal articles suddenly became publishable articles.

The paradigm is a simple pattern, but it is a very important pattern. It works the way our minds work, moving easily from the general to the particular, leading the reader on with effective story-telling. It consists of three parts:

1. A general observation, statement of fact, or question;

2. Followed by a narrowing to a single case;

3. Followed by an example, anecdote, or quote.

The following paragraph is a paradigm in the lead paragraph in an article from *Southern Lady* magazine:

You can usually spot a TaylorG garment. It's a combination of wonderful fabrics, so creatively detailed with buttons, ribbons, and trims, the outfit instantly snatches your attention. "Women want to feel special, and my garments make them look pretty," says Lori Taylor, who founded TaylorG in Dallas, Texas, 11 years ago.

In this paragraph, free-lancer Phyllis Hoffman has used the technique of the paradigm: general observation (You can spot. . .), a narrowing of focus (combination of wonderful fabrics, etc.) and a quote

("Women want to feel special ") Nothing dramatic here, just good, solid magazine writing.

The better and more experienced the writer, the more invisible and seamless the paradigm becomes. In the hands of a seasoned pro, it is open to virtually infinite variation. But whatever form it takes, it is always there.

The freelancer's paradigm is essential to successful non-fiction writing. The writer's job is to hook the reader, lead him through the book, chapter, or article easily and enjoyably, and teach him something useful along the way—all served up with a liberal helping of human interest.

The paradigm enables the writer to do this. It is an antidote to the stale air of abstract fact. It lets the fresh air of personal, one-on-one experience waft through your narrative. In a recent article for *Publishing for Entrepreneurs* magazine, for example, I wanted to get across the idea that anyone with imagination and energy can make money publishing advertising-based local and regional publications. I could have opened my article in a very matter-of-fact way:

> *Periodical publishing on the local and regional level can be quite lucrative. Publishers of tabloids, city magazines and tourism guides regularly make incomes of $100,000 a year and more. Today the typesetting and page layout capabilities of desktop publishing have put such projects within the reach of any entrepreneur who will take the trouble to learn to use them. Statistics reveal . . . .*

Instead, I lead with this paradigm:

The paradigm permits us to sandwich slices of lived experience into otherwise abstract non-fiction narratives.

> *Hometown publishing is a low-cost, high payoff opportunity. I went into this business five years ago with a Mac Plus, two used desks and a laser writer. This year my company will gross $800,000. Next year we expect to top $1,000,000. What I did, you can do, too.*

General observation, particular example, and personal experience. This paradigm-based lead not only tells the story, but whets the reader's appetite for the details to come. The facts are there in both versions, but the paradigm translates them into the language of personal experience and makes them come alive. (The paradigm, by the way, can make a strong lead for a query. It tells an editor a great deal about your slant, your wit, and your writing style.)

Some very successful books are almost entirely constructed of paradigms. This is particularly true of the classic best-sellers in the salesmanship and motivation genre. Napoleon Hill's *Think and Grow Rich*, Zig Ziglar's *See You at the Top*, W. Clement *Stone's Success Through a Positive Mental Attitude* and Dale Carnegie's *How to Win Friends and Influence People* all fit into this category. So do more recent titles such as Wayne Dyer's *Your Erroneous Zones* and, on a somewhat more intellectual level, M. Scott Peck's *The Road Less Traveled*. Not to mention the granddaddy of them all, Norman Vincent Peale's *The Power of Positive Thinking*.

The television news

The evening news could not survive without the paradigm, which flows smoothly from the general observations of the news anchor to the particular and the inevitable sound bite of the individual reporter in place. "Nature is a powerful adversary," the anchor intones from his New York studio. "When disasters strike, no one can withstand them.

The people of Argus, Oklahoma, learned this first hand this afternoon as a devastating tornado ripped through the town. John Johnson has the details." The anchor then asks, "John, what are things like in Argus tonight?" Reporter Johnson appears on the screen, standing before a wrecked mobile home park. "Peter, the people here are just trying to assess the damage and begin to pick up the pieces." He turns to a distraught woman standing beside him. "Mrs. Wiggs, you have lived right here for five years. Now your home is gone. How will you live?"

"We'll just have to go on living the best way we can," Mrs. Wiggs replies bravely. "That's all we can do." Again, the paradigm moves from the general (Nature's Power), to the flesh and blood particulars of Mrs. Wiggs's cabbage patch, and ends with a quote. And it works, every time.

The paradigm appears in the most unlikely places. Even the most esoteric, highbrow authors ignore it at their peril. Take the case of Immanuel Kant and René Descartes. Kant wrote a monumental tome called the *Critique of Pure Reason*. Descartes wrote a slim volume called the *Discourse on Method*. Both writers were brilliant. Both altered the course of the history of ideas. Yet only one of them—Descartes—is widely read, widely quoted, and universally hailed today as the "father of modern philosophy. "Why is this so? It's the power of the paradigm. Kant's book is a dense, virtually impenetrable jungle of thought, a veritable collapsed universe of ideas and analysis. Descartes, on the other hand, starts out with a first person narrative and a fabulous use of the paradigm:

"I always wondered why mathematicians agree on everything but philosophers agree on nothing," Descartes begins. "Then one cold winter—it was 1637, 1 believe—I was holed up in a small room, stoking a pot-bellied stove and trying to keep warm, and I had an idea. What philosophers needed, I decided, was an absolutely universal starting place, a proposition like 'a straight line is the shortest distance between any two points.' But was there any such proposition? I proceeded to doubt every idea in my mind, except for one. I could not doubt that I was doubting. My thought processes proved at least my own existence."

"I think," Descartes concluded, "therefore I am." This is not just good philosophy, it is also a perfect paradigm.

The ATC factor

The book writing system I have outlined in this book is simple. Anyone can do it. It works. I know this from my own experience and from the experience of students to whom I have taught it.

There's only one more step. Turn on your computer, or square your typewriter in front of you, or pull out your legal pad—however you prefer to put words on paper. Push your chair into position. Then sit your rear end down in the chair, consult you first batch of idea slips, and start writing. Don't wait for the perfect moment; don't wait until you know everything you are going to say. Those times will never come.

Writing, like every craft, is hard work. So there's the chair. Unless you sit yourself down upon it and put pen to paper (or fingers to keyboard), you retreat permanently into your dreams.

Richard Rhodes, science writer and biographer and winner of the Pulitzer Prize, tells us that when he asked his mentor, Conrad Knickerbocker how to get a certain piece of writing done, Knickerbocker offered this blunt advice: "Rhodes, you apply ass to chair."

Rhodes had his mentor. I am yours. I have traveled the way you are now traveling. So I take your hand and tell you: "Sit down! Apply ass to chair. Get started now! !"

Your Ideas Are Your Intellectual Capital, Maybe the Only Capital You Need!

The value of an idea? Here's what movie and TV producer Ben Grazer had to say in a recent interview with Fortune Magazine. "My whole career was built on one piece of advice that came from two people: [MCA founder] Jules Stein and [former MCA chairman] Lew Wasserman. In 1975 I was a law clerk at Warner Brothers. I'd spent about a year trying to get a meeting with these two men. Finally, they let me in to see them. They both said, separately, 'In order for you to be in the entertainment business, you have to have leverage. Since you have none—no money, no pedigree—you must create leverage. So you need to write—put what's in your mind on paper. Then you'll own a piece of paper. That's leverage."

"With that advice, I wrote the story that became Splash, which was a fantasy that I had about meeting a mermaid. For years, I sent registered letters to myself—movie concepts and other ideas—so that I had my ideas officially on paper. I have about 1,000 letters in a vault. To this day, I feel that my real power is only that—ideas and the confidence to write them down."

·11·

Coda: Getting Published

THE WORLD OF PUBLISHING can be a mysterious one to those who have not ventured into it one way or another. What's more, what most newcomers to the field *think* they know about it is often fragmentary and often dead wrong. Myths abound. Misleading anecdotal evidence is everywhere. My aim is this chapter is to light the publishing landscape for you—at least a little bit—so that you can begin to find your way around in it, learn what is possible in publishing and what is not, learn what you should and should not do to get your book published. When you need more information than I can provide in this one chapter, I will take care to lead you to it, both through the annotated bibliography that follows the text and through Appendix II, my *Inside Publishing FAQ*.

What happens in publishing?

The words "publisher" and "published" have precise meanings, and they may not be what you think. First of all, understand that a publisher is not a printer and a printer is not a publisher. The publisher has the same relationship with his printer as a housing contractor might have with, say, a plumbing company. The contractor's job is to get the whole house built. The plumber's job is to complete his assigned, small part of a much larger project. In the same way, the printer's job is merely to turn out the physical object—a printed book. The publisher's much larger job is to acquire a manuscript, edit it, design it, physical format, get it printed, and market it and sell it. *Any company that does not do all these things is not, in fact, a publisher.* Publishers routinely do business with many different printers, choosing the one whose equipment is best suited to the job at hand and, consequently, less expensive..

Two ways to get published.

There are, for you as a writer, two ways to get published:

1. You can submit your book to an established trade publisher and let them do (or hope that they will do) all of the things that a publisher does.

2. You can become your own publisher (self-publish) and do all of these things yourself. I have gone both of these routes with several of my books and frankly prefer self-publishing. The book you are now reading is self-published.

The first way: traditional trade publishers

Trade publishers range from the mega houses like Random House and Simon and Schuster, to mid-size publishers like Ten Speed Press and Sentient Publications, the publisher of several of my own books. There experiences were the lifeblood of readable articles. In doing this, I put the structure basic to all good nonfiction writing into "one-two-three" form and gave it a name: the "freelancer's paradigm."

Results were immediate when writers adopted he paradigm. Marginal articles suddenly became publishable articles.

The paradigm is a simple pattern, but it is a very important pattern. It works the way our minds work, moving easily from the general to the particular, leading the reader on with effective story-telling. It consists of three parts:

1. A general observation, statement of fact, or question;

2. Followed by a narrowing to a single case;

3. Followed by an example, anecdote, or quote.

The following paragraph is a paradigm in the lead paragraph in an article from *Southern Lady* magazine:

You can usually spot a TaylorG garment. It's a combination of wonderful fabrics, so creatively detailed with buttons, ribbons, and trims, the outfit instantly snatches your attention. "Women want to feel special, and my garments make them look pretty," says Lori Taylor, who founded TaylorG in Dallas, Texas, 11 years ago.

In this paragraph, free-lancer Phyllis Hoffman has used the technique of the paradigm: general observation (You can spot. . .), a narrowing of focus (combination of wonderful fabrics, etc.) and a quote

("Women want to feel special ") Nothing dramatic here, just good, solid magazine writing.

The better and more experienced the writer, the more invisible and seamless the paradigm becomes. In the hands of a seasoned pro, it is open to virtually infinite variation. But whatever form it takes, it is always there.

The freelancer's paradigm is essential to successful non-fiction writing. The writer's job is to hook the reader, lead him through the book, chapter, or article easily and enjoyably, and teach him something useful along the way—all served up with a liberal helping of human interest.

> The paradigm permits us to sandwich slices of lived experience into otherwise abstract non-fiction narratives.

The paradigm enables the writer to do this. It is an antidote to the stale air of abstract fact. It lets the fresh air of personal, one-on-one experience waft through your narrative. In a recent article for *Publishing for Entrepreneurs* magazine, for example, I wanted to get across the idea that anyone with imagination and energy can make money publishing advertising-based local and regional publications. I could have opened my article in a very matter-of-fact way:

Periodical publishing on the local and regional level can be quite lucrative. Publishers of tabloids, city magazines and tourism guides regularly make incomes of $100,000 a year and more. Today the typesetting and page layout capabilities of desktop publishing have put such projects within the reach of any entrepreneur who will take the trouble to learn to use them. Statistics reveal . . . .

Instead, I lead with this paradigm:

Hometown publishing is a low-cost, high payoff opportunity. I went into this business five years ago with a Mac Plus, two used desks and a laser writer. This year my company will gross $800,000. Next year we expect to top $1,000,000. What I did, you can do, too.

General observation, particular example, and personal experience. This paradigm-based lead not only tells the story, but whets the reader's appetite for the details to come. The facts are there in both versions, but the paradigm translates them into the language of personal experience and makes them come alive. (The paradigm, by the way, can make a strong lead for a query. It tells an editor a great deal about your slant, your wit, and your writing style.)

Some very successful books are almost entirely constructed of paradigms. This is particularly true of the classic best-sellers in the salesmanship and motivation genre. Napoleon Hill's *Think and Grow Rich*, Zig Ziglar's *See You at the Top*, W. Clement *Stone's Success Through a Positive Mental Attitude* and Dale Carnegie's *How to Win Friends and Influence People* all fit into this category. So do more recent titles such as Wayne Dyer's *Your Erroneous Zones* and, on a somewhat more intellectual level, M. Scott Peck's *The Road Less Traveled*. Not to mention the granddaddy of them all, Norman Vincent Peale's *The Power of Positive Thinking*.

The television news

The evening news could not survive without the paradigm, which flows smoothly from the general observations of the news anchor to the particular and the inevitable sound bite of the individual reporter in place. "Nature is a powerful adversary," the anchor intones from his New York studio. "When disasters strike, no one can withstand them.

A Master Speaks

"I had written three other novels before Carrie—*Rage, The Long Walk,* and *The Running Man* were later published. *Rage* is the most troubling of them. *The Long Walk* may be the best of them. But none of them taught me the things I learned from Carrie White. The most important is that the writer's original perception of a character or characters may be as erroneous as the reader's. Running a close second was the realization that stopping a piece of work just because it's hard, either emotionally or imaginatively, is a bad idea. Sometimes you have to go on when you don't feel like it, and sometimes you're doing good work when it feels like all you are managing is to shovel shit from a sitting position."

—Stephen King, *On Writing*

The people of Argus, Oklahoma, learned this first hand this afternoon as a devastating tornado ripped through the town. John Johnson has the details." The anchor then asks, "John, what are things like in Argus tonight?" Reporter Johnson appears on the screen, standing before a wrecked mobile home park. "Peter, the people here are just trying to assess the damage and begin to pick up the pieces." He turns to a distraught woman standing beside him. "Mrs. Wiggs, you have lived right here for five years. Now your home is gone. How will you live?"

"We'll just have to go on living the best way we can," Mrs. Wiggs replies bravely. "That's all we can do." Again, the paradigm moves from the general (Nature's Power), to the flesh and blood particulars of Mrs. Wiggs's cabbage patch, and ends with a quote. And it works, every time.

The paradigm appears in the most unlikely places. Even the most esoteric, highbrow authors ignore it at their peril. Take the case of Immanuel Kant and René Descartes. Kant wrote a monumental tome called the *Critique of Pure Reason*. Descartes wrote a slim volume called the *Discourse on Method*. Both writers were brilliant. Both altered the course of the history of ideas. Yet only one of them—Descartes—is widely read, widely quoted, and universally hailed today as the "father of modern philosophy. "Why is this so? It's the power of the paradigm. Kant's book is a dense, virtually impenetrable jungle of thought, a veritable collapsed universe of ideas and analysis. Descartes, on the other hand, starts out with a first person narrative and a fabulous use of the paradigm:

"I always wondered why mathematicians agree on everything but philosophers agree on nothing," Descartes begins. "Then one cold winter—it was 1637, 1 believe—I was holed up in a small room, stoking a pot-bellied stove and trying to keep warm, and I had an idea. What philosophers needed, I decided, was an absolutely universal starting place, a proposition like 'a straight line is the shortest distance between any two points.' But was there any such proposition? I proceeded to doubt every idea in my mind, except for one. I could not doubt that I was doubting. My thought processes proved at least my own existence."

"I think," Descartes concluded, "therefore I am." This is not just good philosophy, it is also a perfect paradigm.

The ATC factor

The book writing system I have outlined in this book is simple. Anyone can do it. It works. I know this from my own experience and from the experience of students to whom I have taught it.

There's only one more step. Turn on your computer, or square your typewriter in front of you, or pull out your legal pad—however you prefer to put words on paper. Push your chair into position. Then sit your rear end down in the chair, consult you first batch of idea slips, and start writing. Don't wait for the perfect moment; don't wait until you know everything you are going to say. Those times will never come.

Writing, like every craft, is hard work. So there's the chair. Unless you sit yourself down upon it and put pen to paper (or fingers to keyboard), you retreat permanently into your dreams.

Richard Rhodes, science writer and biographer and winner of the Pulitzer Prize, tells us that when he asked his mentor, Conrad Knickerbocker how to get a certain piece of writing done, Knickerbocker offered this blunt advice: "Rhodes, you apply ass to chair."

Rhodes had his mentor. I am yours. I have traveled the way you are now traveling. So I take your hand and tell you: "Sit down! Apply ass to chair. Get started now! !"

Your Ideas Are Your Intellectual Capital, Maybe the Only Capital You Need!

The value of an idea? Here's what movie and TV producer Ben Grazer had to say in a recent interview with Fortune Magazine. "My whole career was built on one piece of advice that came from two people: [MCA founder] Jules Stein and [former MCA chairman] Lew Wasserman. In 1975 I was a law clerk at Warner Brothers. I'd spent about a year trying to get a meeting with these two men. Finally, they let me in to see them. They both said, separately, 'In order for you to be in the entertainment business, you have to have leverage. Since you have none—no money, no pedigree—you must create leverage. So you need to write—put what's in your mind on paper. Then you'll own a piece of paper. That's leverage."

"With that advice, I wrote the story that became Splash, which was a fantasy that I had about meeting a mermaid. For years, I sent registered letters to myself—movie concepts and other ideas—so that I had my ideas officially on paper. I have about 1,000 letters in a vault. To this day, I feel that my real power is only that—ideas and the confidence to write them down."

·11·

CODA: GETTING PUBLISHED

THE WORLD OF PUBLISHING can be a mysterious one to those who have not ventured into it one way or another. What's more, what most newcomers to the field *think* they know about it is often fragmentary and often dead wrong. Myths abound. Misleading anecdotal evidence is everywhere. My aim is this chapter is to light the publishing landscape for you—at least a little bit—so that you can begin to find your way around in it, learn what is possible in publishing and what is not, learn what you should and should not do to get your book published. When you need more information than I can provide in this one chapter, I will take care to lead you to it, both through the annotated bibliography that follows the text and through Appendix II, my *Inside Publishing FAQ.*

What happens in publishing?

The words "publisher" and "published" have precise meanings, and they may not be what you think. First of all, understand that a publisher is not a printer and a printer is not a publisher. The publisher has the same relationship with his printer as a housing contractor might have with, say, a plumbing company. The contractor's job is to get the whole house built. The plumber's job is to complete his assigned, small part of a much larger project. In the same way, the printer's job is merely to turn out the physical object—a printed book. The publisher's much larger job is to acquire a manuscript, edit it, design it, physical format, get it printed, and market it and sell it. *Any company that does not do all these things is not, in fact, a publisher.* Publishers routinely do business with many different printers, choosing the one whose equipment is best suited to the job at hand and, consequently, less expensive..

Two ways to get published.

There are, for you as a writer, two ways to get published:

1. You can submit your book to an established trade publisher and let them do (or hope that they will do) all of the things that a publisher does.

2. You can become your own publisher (self-publish) and do all of these things yourself. I have gone both of these routes with several of my books and frankly prefer self-publishing. The book you are now reading is self-published.

The first way: traditional trade publishers

Trade publishers range from the mega houses like Random House and Simon and Schuster, to mid-size publishers like Ten Speed Press and Sentient Publications, the publisher of several of my own books. There

or title pages of books you may have written on the subject.

6. *Ask for a response.* You may consider it obvious to the editor reading your query that you are asking him to make a decision. That may be so, but my experience on both sides of the editorial desk tells me that things go better when you specifically ask for a decision. Thus my query to Esquire ended with the phrase: "I can begin work on this project immediately." My *Desktop Publisher* query ended more explicitly, "May I send you an outline and sample chapters?"

7. *Mistakes to avoid.* While the following gaffes may seem very elementary, I see them very frequently in the queries that I read. When you make them your query is dead in the water.

- Do not include a paragraph telling how much Aunt Minnie and Uncle Ted think of your idea and how they encouraged you to send the query in.

- Avoid self-evaluation. Do not inform the editor that you are sure that your book or article is "just what your readers have been waiting for" and that you feel certain that "everyone will be excited by it." You may well feel this way, but leave such judgments up to the editor.

- Don't submit your query on fancy, colored paper. It's white bond and white bond only, and of standard 11.5 by 11 size.

- Always include a self-addressed, stamped envelope.

The book proposal

If your query finds favor and your target editor asks for more, you will send in a book proposal. The real meat of your book proposal is in the three sample chapters you send along, but there is some preliminary stuff you also need to do.

1. Give your book as strong a title and log line as you can come up with. (A log line is a one sentence sell line describing your book). Follow this with a one or two paragraph summary.

2. Estimate the length of your book in terms of the number of words you think it will take to cover the topic.

3. Describe any special art, graphs, illustrations that you will include

4. Provide a full table of contents, telling what is contained in each chapter as well as the chapter head. Keep this succinct but compelling.

5. Describe your target readership. Tell why you think your book is a viable addition to its field. Develop its market potential.

6. Analyze four or five competing books. List each by title, author, publisher, the year publication, the number of pages and the price. Describe each book. How is yours different? Better?

7. Tell about your background and promotional skills. What will you personally contribute to the sales and marketing mix of your book? Are you a good speaker, a radio personality, the owner of a popular blog?

8. Provide the first chapter and two additional chapters, double spaced and in standard manuscript format. As in any manuscript, put the book title and page number in the upper right hand corner

of the page. Don't neglect to send a cover letter reminding whoever opens your proposal packet that you are sending it in answer to a request and tell the reader who made the request.

The contract.

If you are successful in your query and your proposal, you will be offered a contract. Study it carefully, for there are many clauses that can greatly affect your rights to profit from your work. Is there an advance against royalties? What are the royalties and when are they paid? What about electronic rights? How are book club rights, foreign rights and other subsidiary rights shared?

These are only a few of the questions that you must ask and whose answers you must completely understand. Fortunately, there is a good, thorough manual to lead you through your publishing agreement. It is a book by Martin Levin called *Be Your Own Literary Agent* (Ten Speed Press). Levin's book is the best I know on publishing contracts. It will spare you much grief and possibly make you a good deal more money. Not that anybody makes much money in publishing (unless they are Stephen King, J. K. Rowling or an ax murderer with a first rate ghost writer).

Option two: publish it yourself

The second route to getting your book in print is to publish it yourself. In case there's any lingering doubt in your mind concerning the legitimacy of self-publication, let me set the record straight. Writers and others who have not been following the revolutionary changes in the publishing industry in the last few years may not be aware of the way in which the landscape has changed. Almost forty years ago now, Bill Henderson, founder of Pushcart Press, self-published his *The Publish-It-Yourself Handbook: Literary Tradition and How-To (Pushcart Press)*. This book was a rousing success and sold edition after edition nationwide. Sales of this one title were adequate to build Henderson's one-man enterprise (Pushcart Press) into one of the success stories in the independent publishing movement of recent years. Henderson was a man before his time. When he wrote his *Handbook,* the technology that has now put self-publishing within easy reach of anyone who truly wishes to get into print had not been invented. So the how-to part of his book is dated. The "literary tradition" section, however, did a great service for the whole independent publishing movement. Henderson pointed out that self-publication had a long, distinguished history. Walt Whitman, Carl Sandburg, Stephen Crane, Edgar Allen Poe, and dozens of other great writers self-published at one time or another. So did I. So can you.

Far from being a back door through which one sneaks into the world of publishing, self-publication today is *very* respectable. Publishing pros—editors and marketers of some of the biggest publishing houses—routinely recommend self-publishing to writers with good, solid books that are not likely destined for best-sellerdom. As money becomes tighter and as major publishers focus more and more exclusively on the quest for blockbuster best sellers, it has become inescapably clear that for books with strong but not enormous sales potential, self-publication may be the only alternative. Judith Appelbaum, a long-time pro in the New York publishing field, is the author of a book called *How to Get Happily Published*. Appelbaum tells writers how to approach the larger commercial houses, but also devotes a very generous portion of the book to the how-to of self-publication. Among many others, this New York pro has no hesitation in treating self-publication as a perfectly feasible and totally acceptable alternative for writers. Neither do I. I have found self-publication just satisfying and considerably more profitable than traditional publication.

The technology that makes it possible.

Recent developments in the technology of book design, layout and printing make self-publication both financially and technically feasible for any writer. If you already own a computer, and if you are willing to learn how to do some of the work yourself, you can get started with an outlay of just a few hundred dollars.

The first of these developments is that of the hyper-powerful desktop computers we all use today, along with typesetting and book design software developed by companies like Adobe. Their *InDesign* software, along with a word processing program like Microsoft Word, will easily handle the work of writing and design. My computer also gives me instant access to the incredible power of Internet communications. As recently as 1995 I had to ask someone to explain to me what the Internet was. Today, it is the backbone of my entire business. All this means that you—anyone—can organize a publishing company with worldwide sales from a small office in your home. My office consists of a 300 square foot area in a remodeled garage. From this tiny office I sell books around the world.

The second technological development is that of digital printing. Over the past ten years companies like Xerox have developed printers capable of printing and binding high quality paperback books with a full color cover in just minutes, in one operation, using no printing plates and no printing presses. By utilizing this technology any self-publisher can very affordably print enough books to send out for review and to test the market. At the moment I am getting this book ready to market. It has 160 pages, is perfect bound and has a glossy color cover. After paying a set up fee of $70, the digital printing will cost just $3.25 per book. I ordered fifty books to send to reviewers and buyers for just $162.50. Just a decade ago I would have had to order a couple of thousand books at a cost of $3000 or more before I had any idea whether or not the book would sell.

Do these two things to become your own publisher

There is nothing difficult about setting up as your own publisher. To get started you must do just two things, name your publishing company and buy a block of ISBN numbers (See Appendix II).

1. *Name Your Publishing Company.* Do not name your company after yourself. Choose something else. Publishing one's own books is a respectable business these days, but you don't have to rub the reader's nose—or the book buyers for the bookstore chains—in that fact. You may not want the same name appearing on the title page as author and, at the bottom, as publisher, although I did it with this book. Whatever you do, don't choose a name that belittles your newborn publishing company. I don't think I would go for "Last Chance Press" or "Better Than Nothing Books," for instance.

2. *Get your block of ISBN numbers.* Every published book has an *international standard book number*, or ISBN, on the copyright page and

on the back cover. The ISBN identifies both the book itself and the publisher of the book. You buy these numbers on the web site of the R.R. Bowker Company, the administrator of the ISBN system in the United States (http://www.isbn.org/standards). The cost is about $250 for a block of ten numbers..

That's all there is to it. Do these things, and you're a publisher. Now all you've got to do is publish your book. There are several manuals on the market that will help you do this, or which the most widely used is Dan Poynter's *Self Publishers Manual*, now in its tenth edition. Another helpful book is *The Publishing Game,* by Fern Reiss. Reiss tends to hype up the process a bit, but the info she gives is reliable and set out in a helpful 1, 2, 3, format. These two books should be all you need to plan your way into self-publishing. You will find a great deal more helpful information on book design, typography, and marketing in Appendix II of this book.

The POD confusion: pay careful attention

Publishers large and small quickly adopted digital printing when it became available. The digital printing process is one of the few to-good-to be-true things that actually turned out to be true. Advance review copies are routinely produced digitally by almost everyone, and even the most distinguished university presses utilize it to publish small editions of highly specialized books and to keep older books in print after initial inventories are exhausted. It is no longer necessary to keep physical books stored in warehouses. They can be kept available digitally forever, incurring no cost whatsoever. This digital manufacturing process was soon dubbed "print on demand," since it permitted the printing of even a single book to fill a single order. The phrase "print on demand" was soon reduced to its initials, POD. This has led to a major, and if not understood, a potentially disastrous confusion for self-publishers.

Prospective self-publishers must clearly understand the two very different senses in this acronym is used. We have just learned that digital, POD printing, is one of the things that makes self-publishing possible for almost anyone. But beware. The POD designation has also been appropriated as a general name for firms, usually operating on-line, that describe themselves as "POD Publishers." Publishing with a so-called "POD publisher" is not self-publishing and can sometimes be worse than not publishing at all.

How and why is this true? Let's a mythical company called WePublish.Com as a model "POD publisher." WePublish.Com invites writers to send in their books. WePublish.Com promises to "publish" these books, formatting the interior and designing a cover at what seems an affordable price. Little or no editing is done. These interior and cover designs are formatted, fitting into standard templates. WePublish.Com is the publisher of record for your book. It assigns an ISBN to the work published and has a contract with author specifying royalties to be paid on retail sales and income sharing on sales of subsidiary rights—if any retail sales or rights sales do in fact occur. WePublish.Com promises to make the author's book "available" in bookstores and other outlets. Note that this does not mean that the books will actually on the shelf. It simply means that the author's book will be listed in the Books-in-Print database and so available for special order whenever a customer asks for such an order. There is not likely to be any promotion to make the reading public in general aware of the availability of the book. Worse, because WePublish.Com is not selective in what it publishes, busy reviewers do not give its books more than a glance, if that.

When it does print books, WePublish.Com uses print-on-demand technology. WePublish.Com does not own printing equipment, but farms its printing work out to Lightning Source. So how does WePublish.Com make money? It sells printed books directly to its authors at discounts ranging from 40% to 50% of the retail price, which is usually set artificially high. Let's say that the print version of your book retails for $19.95 and is sold to the author at a 40% discount, or $11.97. If this hypothetical book has 200 pages, the printing, at the very most, costs WePublish.Com $3.90 and probably less. Thus WePublish.Com nets a profit of $8.07 on books sold to its own authors. Let's say, further, that WePublish.Com publishes 1000 authors (they actually publish far more) each month, each of whom orders 25 copies of his or her book for friends, relatives, and local reviewers, then the income is substantial. One thousand multiplied by 25 equals 25,000. This figure multiplied by $8.07 equals $201, 750. This produces an annual income of $2,421,000. When you consider that WePublish.Com, since it is a print-on-demand publisher, has no investment in inventory and probably no investment in printing presses, and that the whole enterprise, once set up, can do business almost entirely in the thin air of hyperspace, the net profit is substantial.

Whatever happens, WePublish.Com wins, but the author almost always loses.

APPENDIX I
CONTACTS AND SOURCES

Books

The books listed below are few in number but solid in content. Each of them has been a valuable source of information and inspiration for me in setting up and managing my publishing businesses. Each contains concrete, usable information and techniques that can make you money. I highly recommend them to you.

AP Stylebook and Libel Manual. Almost everything you need to know about newspaper style is contained in this book. It can become a valuable manual which sets specific style standards for all your publications. It is inexpensive and can be furnished to everyone in your editorial department. It is great for magazine free-lancers. Highly topical and practical. Great style guide for magazine writing.

The Chicago Manual of Style. University of Chicago Press. This utterly complete handbook is as close to an industry standard (for American usage) as any. It should be on every writer's bookshelf. Academic (scholarly) writers may prefer the Modern Language Association Stylebook, and social scientists sometimes prefer the American Psychological Association Stylebook. The Chicago manual is the big one, however, and the most generally accepted. Indispensable.

Haldeman-Julius, Emmanuel. *The First Hundred Million.* This is a personal favorite. Newspaperman-publisher Haldeman-Julius tells the fascinating story of the creation of his "Little Blue Book" series.

The Blue Books were simple, saddle-stitched pamphlets containing reprints of the classics as well as practical information on such then-taboo topics as sex education for women. Everyone interested in the publishing and book world should treat themselves to a read of this book. There is a great chapter on the "Book Hospital" to which he consigned titles that were not selling well, tinkered with the title, and transformed them into profitable publications. If you think the choice of a title is unimportant, this chapter will change your mind. This chapter is also available on my website at www.PubMart.com.

Henderson, Bill. *The Publish-It-Yourself Handbook*. Harper & Row, New York, NY. 1987. Henderson presents a dozen or more essays by literary writers and poets telling how they took charge of their own careers and published their own work and, often, the works of others as well. Inspiring and reassuring. You really ought to read it.

Kremer, John. *1001 Ways to Market Your Books*. Open Horizons. 1001 Ways is a great idea-generator. When sales on one of my books are languishing, I browse through Kremer. Almost always, I will discover an avenue I have not explored, or something Kremer says will bring another, related idea to mind. An excellent resource for anyone selling books.

Levin, Martin P. *Be Your Own Literary Agent*: *The Ultimate, Insider's Guide to Getting Published*. Ten Speed Press. The best book ever written on freelance agreements, book contracts, and the opportunities, perils and pitfalls of doing business as a writer. Highly recommended.

Lukeman, Noah. *The First Five Pages*. An agent offers valuable insight into stylistic flaws that prompt an agent or an editor to toss a submission aside rather than read it through. Highly recommended

Masterson, Pete. *Book Design and Production: A Guide for Authors and Publishers*. Aeonix Publishing Group. Covers book design from A to Z. Thorough and reliable, based on the author's decades of experience in the book business. Step-by-step instructions on using InDesign to do interior book design and layout. You need this one in your personal reference library.

Poynter, Dan. *The Self-Publishing Manual*. Para Publishing. A thorough how-to guide to the self-publication and marketing of adult nonfiction. Much of the information is also of use to literary publishers. The standard in the field.

Williams, Thomas A. *Poet Power: The Practical Poet's Complete Guide to Getting Published*. Sentient Publications. Covers everything form magazine publication to self-publication to the design and publication of chapbooks. A very practical and highly detailed manual.

A Writer's Guide to Copyright. Poets & Writers, Inc. It may be hard to believe, but few writers are really familiar with copyright law, which is more complicated than you may expect, what with revision of the copyright act, exceptions to these revisions, extensions of terms, etc. This book will tell you what you want (and need) to know.

Magazines

Poets and Writers Magazine. Poets & Writers, Inc., 72 Spring Street, New York, NY 10012. Published bimonthly. The best of all magazines for poets and literary authors. Brilliantly edited. Not only a great read, but useful, too. lists hundreds of available grants for literary prose writers and poets

Publishers Weekly. PW, as it is called, is the trade magazine of the publishing industry. If you are interested in the business of books, subscribe for a year and try it out. Or go to the PW website: publishersweekly.com.

The Writer. Kalmbach Publishing Company. Published monthly. An old-timer in the field, now with new editorial direction, the magazine publishes articles on the craft of writing from authors who have risen to prominence in the field.

Writer's Digest. Probably the most widely-read magazine for writers, Writer's Digest has something of a split personality, combining useful articles on the craft with large numbers of advertisements for "editorial service" and "poetry contests" that one would do well to check out carefully, since many are scams of one sort or another.

Directories and Guides

American Book Trade Directory. R. R. Bowker, 121 Chanlon Road, New Providence, NJ 07974. Lists of bookstores and retail outlets, along with distributors and wholesalers.

American Library Directory. R. R. Bowker, 121 Chanlon Road, New Providence, NJ 07974. Public and school libraries. Each entry also indicates the monies allotted for new purchases.

Bacon's Publicity Checker. Bacon's, 332 South Michigan Avenue, Chicago, IL 60604. Updated annually.

Bacon's Radio/TV Directory. Bacon's, 332 South Michigan Avenue, Chicago, IL 60604. Updated annually.

Gebbies All-In-One Directory. Gebbie Press. This is an easy-to-use directory of magazines, newspapers, and radio and TV stations. It is also available as an electronic mailing list. You can get the information you need at www.gebbie.com.

The International Directory of Little Magazines and Small Presses. Dustbooks, P.O. Box 100, Paradise, CA 95967; 800-477-6110.

Literary Market Place. R. R. Bowker, 121 Chanlon Road, New Providence, NJ 07974. Updated annually. Usually referred to simply as LMP, Literary Market Place is the most complete directory of all persons and organizations associated with the publishing business: publishing houses and their specialties, editors, agents, book clubs, manufacturers, suppliers, etc. A new edition is published each year. While addresses may not change rapidly, the names of editors do change. Always use the latest issue available to you.

Organizations and Networking

There are two organizations for independent publishers. These are the Independent Publishers Association (formerly the Publishers Marketing Association) at http://www.pma.com and the Small Publishers Association of North America (SPAN) at http://www.spannet.org/. Membership is inexpensive and both organizations publish very helpful newsletters.

If you live in New York, Los Angeles, or San Francisco, "local" also means "national." But in every town of any size there guilds, clubs and associations for writers and poets. They offer everything from moral support to publication opportunities and everything in between: conferences, critique groups, workshops and competitions.

In Savannah, Ga., where I now live, there is a very active writing community, but no organization of practicing writers. I am now in the process of forming one.

Before that, I lived in Coral Springs, a suburb of Fort Lauderdale, Florida. Just to the north was the Poets of the Palm Beaches club. In Miami, to the south, was the National Writer's Association, South Florida Chapter. There is the Palm Beach Book Fest in the Spring and the Miami Book Fair in the Fall, both of which draw name novelists, poets, dramatists, and journalists as speakers and as attendees.

In North Carolina, where I spent many years teaching and publishing magazines, there is the statewide North Carolina Writers Network, with its headquarters in the Chapel Hill-Carrboro area, as well as writers' clubs in the towns where I lived.

Appendix 2
Tom's Inside Publishing FAQ

Q. What is an agent, and how do you get one?

A. Agents are quasi-mythical creatures, more often spoken of than seen, said to inhabit the downtown labyrinths of New York, Los Angeles, and a few other major metropolitan centers. Writers have been known to spend endless hours trying to capture one. This is because, for fiction writers, agents are a virtual necessity if you want a trade publisher to publish your book. For non-fiction writers, working through an agent can be very helpful but is not an absolute necessity

There are three things you have got to understand if you want an agent to represent you.

 1. What a good agent does

 2. Why he does it, and,

 3. How, given these facts, you contrive to get his or her attention and enter into a mutually profitable relationship.

An agent, contrary to the beliefs of may writers, cannot afford to work virtually *pro bono* for writers whose books have little chance of success in the market place—and by success I mean sales success, success in moving off bookstore shelves and into the hands of consumers. An agent may or may not love your book, love the literary world, or even love writers. Like you, the agent has a mortgage payment and a car payment, kids to send to school, doctor bills, braces—all the expenses that the rest of us have. Except that since the agent lives in New York or maybe Los Angeles, so his bills are even higher than ours. If he does not bring home the bacon—and a fairly large slab of it at that—he is soon in big financial trouble. Literary agenting is not a business for the weak of heart. One who engages in it has little time to waste in unproductive effort. An agent lives by his wits. He is not salaried, has no company retirement fund, no sick leave, no paid-for hospitalization. He banks on two things, and two things only, to pay his bills:

1. His ability to pick from the many thousands of books submitted to his agency each year those few that he thinks he can sell, and,

2. His intimate knowledge of the publishing business, of who is looking for what, of the current needs of as many publishing houses as he can gather information about. The agent must choose books that not only get published but which sell in large numbers after they are published. That is because an agent lives by commissions alone, getting (usually) fifteen percent of the royalties that the author earns. If the author earns little or nothing, the agent also earns little or nothing.

Q. What will happen when my book is published?

A. Nothing will happen unless you make it happen. This is true whether you are published by a traditional house on a royalty basis or whether you self-publish. Yes, you are able to give freshly printed copies to your family and friends. You can take copies to the next meeting of your writers' club and put them out on the "member's books" table for everyone to see and admire. But such pleasures do not put money in your back account, get books on the bookstore shelves (and off of them via sales), or transform you overnight into overnight celebrity. When such things — or at least some of them — do happen, they do so as the result of hard work, in part by the publisher but mostly by the author. What a publisher can do is limited by time, money, and their own self-interest. The work of getting visibility for your book, getting it reviewed and getting it sold is slow, painstaking, and constant. It must be carried on relentlessly by taking advantage of every single opportunity for promotion that comes your way. Small publishers do not have time, staff, or resources to keep up day-to-day promotion over the long haul, and the big publishers, bringing out dozens or even hundreds of titles a year typically abandon those of their titles that do not quickly rise to the top in sales.

Q. I hear talk about the "big New York publishers" and the "small, independent publishers." What's the difference?

A. There are two ways to make money in publishing:

1.Sell many thousands of books, making a small net profit from each

2. Sell far fewer books and make a somewhat larger profit from each.

The "big publishers," because of their corporate and financial structure, go the first of these routes. The smaller publishers and self-publishers, because of their lower overhead and operating expenses, can make a go of it if they are successful in moving just five to ten thousand books, and sometimes even fewer than that.

This split was not always the case. Not too many years ago, even the major publishing houses began as an enterprise of one or two individuals. Dick Simon and Max Schuster *were* Simon and Schuster. Alfred Knopf was Knopf. Bennett Cerf was Random House. Publishing was a highly personal and even a romantic business.

Those days are gone forever. Conglomerates like Bertlemann's in Germany, or Rupert Murdoch, or Time-Warner have been on buying sprees, acquiring the old companies as the founding owners began to grow old and cash out. Everybody in big-publisher land is owned by someone else. Book publishing has become a part of high finance, and in high finance the bottom line is the only thing that counts. (On the subject of this question, see *The Blockbuster Complex* by Thomas Whiteside., and *The Making of a Bestseller*, by Arthur T. Vanderbilt)

Enter the "small, independent publisher" of recent years (and I include self-publishers in this category). The centralization of big-time publishing has opened a viable space for the small guys to bring out good, niche market books that can turn a limited, if more or less precarious, profit on sales of just a few thousand copies. Print on Demand technology, such as that provided by Lightning Source (LaVergne, TN) has greatly reduced the amount of money such publishers have to spend to get a book out and for sale. Moreover, the recent rise of Ebook publishing may one day offer enormous new opportunities for the independents. I say "may offer" because Ebook publishers are still, as I write this, looking for an effective way to promote and sell their products.

Q. I have heard that most books sold in the United States are sold in the stores of three or four big chains. Is this true?

A. I'm afraid it is. Bookstores have joined the trend toward "bigger is better." Many small, individually operated bookstores have been forced to close because they could not meet the competition of the "superstores" like Borders, Barnes & Noble, and Books-a-Million. These stores now account for almost three quarters of book sales annually in this country. The dominant role of the chain stores has increased to the point that, believe it or not, editors at publishing companies sometimes sound out chain store buyers before deciding to publish or not to publish and otherwise worthy book. I have done that with this book.

Q. What about Amazon.com and other on-line retailers?

A. Amazon.com is the most important of the on-line booksellers and one of largest booksellers overall. Many self-publishers who find it difficult to get on the shelves of the chain bookstores use Amazon as their main source of single copy sales. To do this successfully requires that you get to know and learn to utilize the many marketing features that Amazon provides to every publisher of every book on its immense site. Indeed, there are entire books focusing on this very subject. Aaron Shepard's book *Aiming at Amazon* is the best of these, and I highly recommend that you get it and study it. I had been selling books on Amazon for several years before reading Aiming at Amazon, and still discovered that there was much I did not know in the pages of this book. Aaron Shephard also posts frequent updates to chronicle the ever-changing, ever-developing Amazon.Com marketplace on his web site, www.aaronshep.com/. Here are some things to do.

1. *Help buyers find your book.* One way to get more Amazon sales is to do everything you can to make sure that your book comes up on the screen before those of your competitors. While there is no way to guarantee that it will, there is much you can do to make this more likely. On of these things is to give your book a subtitle that contains as many search-sensitive words as possible. When I put this book on Amazon, I will give it a subtitle like "A Writer's Guide to Generating Ideas, Organizing Data, and Writing Non-Fiction Books, Business Books, Theses and Dissertations." You don't have to use this rambling subtitle on your printed books, but you can use it on Amazon to help your title come up for browsers in all these categories. You can also add "tags" to a book. Scroll down on your book's detail page and find "tags that customers associate with this produce." Just below you will see a window that permits you to "add tags." For *How to Write a Book*, I might enter the tags writing, authorship, writer, ideas, how to write, thesis, dissertation, business writing, and doubtless many more.

2. *Add content.* Go to http://www.Amazon.com/publishers page.

There you will find a link to an "add content" This is wide open to you to add whatever info you think might help sell your book. Non-fiction books always need detailed tables of contents. Here is the sample of the first chapter in the table of contents of my book *How to Publish Your Magazine, Guidebook or Weekly Newspaper* as it appears on the book detail page on Amazon.com.

1. Entrepreneurial Publishing: An Overview / 4

The Publishing Revolution • A One-Person Business • The "Sweat-of-Your-Brow (SOB) Factor" • Getting into Publishing • How I Got into Publishing •The First Big Project • Brains, Time and Energy—No Money Up Front • Moonlighting • The Three Secrets of Success

Other helpful Amazon features include "search inside the book (SIB), which makes several pages of your book available to the Amazon browser. Amazon also invites customers to write reviews of the books they purchase. Make sure that all favorable reviews that come to your attention are posted on your book's detail page. You can add these yourself and have those that know you and your book write them.

On-line book sales, bestsellers aside, are not likely to be dramatic. A good non-fiction book may sell a dozen or so copies a month through Amazon and several more on other Internet sites, including your own web site.

Q. So the chains and Amazon have centralized bookselling. Has the distribution of books also been centralized?

A. Yes, the distribution of books has become as highly centralized as bookselling has. Not too many years ago, "book travelers,"— commissioned salespeople who represented one or more publishers—used to crisscross the country making direct sales calls on hundreds of small bookstores, presenting the crop of new titles for the coming season. This system was colorful but ultimately cumbersome and inefficient, and by the 1960s book travelers were being replaced by a far smaller number of book distributors and wholesalers, who made it possible for stores and libraries to order all their books at one time and from one or two suppliers. Their bookkeeping was immensely simplified and made almost automatic. Their costs were cut. The advent of desktop computers vastly accelerated this trend. Bar codes could now be scanned and sales and inventory needs instantly calculated. Giant wholesalers like the Ingram Book Company and Baker & Taylor are now able to handle hundreds of thousands of orders with great efficiency, both for themselves and for their clients. These two wholesalers buy their books from companies called "book distributors," each of which represents many individual publishers. The following two entries go further into this subject.

Q. What are the consequences for publishers of the current distribution system?

A. What was good for bookstores was not necessarily good for publishers, and wound up taking a big bite out of the publisher's bottom line. There was a new link in the chain from publisher to bookstore: the distributor. Distributors also had to get their slice of the already meager publishing pie. It has become now almost impossible for publishers to get their books into bookstores across the country without using the services of a distributor. Chain bookstores will not order directly from a publisher. After bookstore discounts, wholesaler's discounts and distributor's discounts, a publisher can wind up will as little as 23 to 27 percent of the retail price of his products. And out of that amount the publisher must pay all expenses—acquisition, editing, design and printing, marketing, royalties—and still make a profit if he wants to stay in business. That is why many small publishers—and self-publishers, if they are wise—concentrate on niche market books that can be sold directly to consumers through direct mail, web sites and other means that bypass the distribution system.

Q. Can you clarify all book distribution levels and what happens at each of them?

A. There are variations on the theme, but here are the basics.

1. *Direct sales from the publisher:* The publisher sells some books directly to consumers through web sites, book fairs and in other ways. These are the most profitable sales, since there are no middle men (persons?) to take a cut of the profits.

2. *Sales by the publisher directly to bookstores.* The publisher can sell wholesale to bookstores, which will then make the books available for retail sales. The publisher pays a discount ranging from 10% to 40% off the cover price to bookstores, depending on the quantity of books that the store orders. Most sales directly to bookstores are onsies and twosies, in response to special customer orders. Large orders for stocking books are not likely through this channel.

3. *Sales by the publisher to wholesalers,* who then sell books to bookstores. Most bookstores, and all of the chains, prefer to order books from wholesalers such as Ingram Books and Baker & Taylor Books. Knowing this, the publisher makes books available to the wholesalers at a typical discount of 55% off the cover price. The problem is, it is sometimes difficult for the small publisher to do business with the wholesalers unless he has a distributor.

4. *Thus, the distributors enter the picture.* Distributors sell the publisher's books to the chain stores and to the wholesalers. The chains buy mostly from wholesalers. Wholesalers buy mostly from distributors. It is all very confusing, but the upshot is that if you are counting on selling a lot of books through major bookstores, you can't do without a distributor. The publisher must give a discount of 63%, sometimes

more, to the distributor. This is a severe blow to both the publisher, who pays the discount, and the author, whose royalties are more and more frequently based on "monies actually received" by the publisher after all discounts have been paid. This system is expensive and not generally effective for niche market books that sell in limited numbers.

Q. I self-published my book. Can I get a distributor?

A. You can, if two things happen:

1. The distributor thinks that your book is likely to sell well, and (

2. You have other books coming down the line.

Distributors are looking for books that will generate a profit for their business. This means that you've got to have a solid, well-designed, competitively-priced book. You may also have to convince your prospective distributor that you are not a "one book" publisher, that other titles will soon follow the one you are presenting to them.

I once called on a well-heeled acquaintance who ran a small manufacturing company to ask him to buy a 25% share in the community weekly newspaper I was then publishing. I would use the money, I said, to tide the business over until it was more profitable. I added that it would be "very good for the community" if he would do so. My friend looked at me, stroked his chin, as said, "Tom, the first thing you've got to learn about business is that money is not sentimental." I have never forgotten that lesson. Book distributors cannot afford to be sentimental, either. Selling books is a tough job, and they have to be careful which books they take on. Their companies go belly-up every year.

You can do a search on the Internet to find a list of distributors. Two good places to look are http://www.bookzone.com and the "publishers resources" page at http://www.execpc.com. Choose two or three and check them out by asking for a list of their clients. Contact some of those clients to ask how things are going. Do they recommend their distributor to others? Do they pay on time? Are their any signs of financial instability? Settle on one of them and make your pitch.

The distributor will be interested in doing an on-going business with you. If this is your first book, let them know about plans for any others that will be coming along later. If the distributor thinks he can make money selling your book, he will adopt it. If he thinks your book is badly designed (you typeset the interior to save money although you know very little about typesetting, and your Aunt Minnie drew a picture for the cover); if he thinks there is no market for your subject matter; if he thinks that your book is badly written; if he thinks that it is not priced right for the market; if he thinks you will never publish another book — for any of these and many other reasons he may send your book back to you with a "Thanks, but no thanks" letter.

Q. I have a distributor. When will he pay me for the books I sent in.

A. The distributor will not pay you until he sells your books. But even this is not as clean-cut as it sounds. Here's the way it works. You send your books, one or two thousand of them, to your distributor. He advertises them in his next catalog. His salespeople go out and make presentations to wholesalers, chain bookstores and, in some cases, to independent bookstores. Some of these people order copies of your book. These orders are fulfilled. So far, no money has changed hands at all. You have sent your books to the distributor on consignment and he sends them along to the people who have ordered them on consignment. As bookstores and wholesalers sell books, they pay the distributor for them at their discounted rate. (We may now be twelve months or more down the road.) After he receives payment from his costumers, your distributor, as specified in your contract, sends you a check for your share of the receipts. But not all of your share. He typically holds some of your funds back to cover the cost of potential returns. The distributor charges these returns back against the funds he has withheld from your check. The bookkeeping is messy, and you have to keep a sharp eye on operations and a sharper eye on inventory control in place to make sure that you eventually get all the money that is coming to you.

Q. What is a "barcode," and how do I get one?

A. The concept of the barcode was patented in 1952 but had to wait twenty years until the technology that underlies the point of purchase scanning of products was finally developed. It is said that the first bar code scan at a cash register occurred in the mid-seventies with the purchase of a ten-cent pack of Juicy Fruit chewing gum. The Universal Product Code (UPC) barcode is used for most merchandise, including the mass market paperbacks that are often sold on grocery store and other magazine/book racks. The EAN barcode (European Article Number) is used for all other books. This barcode may simply record the ISBN number of the book or it may also include the price of the book. This is called a "price extension."

Q, What is an ISBN number?

A. ISBN is an abbreviation for "International Standard Book Number." Every book published needs one of these, obtained from the R. R. Bowker Company. The ISBN system originated when W. H. Smith, a major British bookseller decided to change over to a computerized warehouse in 1967 and wanted a standard numbering system for books it carried. Consultants were hired to work on behalf of W.H. Smith, the British Publishers Association's Distribution and Methods Committee and others in the U.K. book trade. They devised the Standard Book Numbering (ISBN) system in 1966, and it was implemented in 1967. In 1969 this system was approved by the International Organization for Standardization (ISO) as a universal system, and implemented in 1970. Books published before this time do not have ISBNs. The R.R. Bowker company administers the ISBN system in the United States. Though ISBN numbers used to be assigned to publishers at no charge, publishers now must purchase "blocks" of ISBN numbers from Bowker by going to http://www.isbn.org. As this is written, a block of ten numbers costs $275; 100 numbers cost $995; and 1000 numbers cost $1750.

The ISBN number is printed in digital and 'human readable" form on the copyright page and the back cover of paperback books, and on the copyright page, front dust cover flap and the back cover of casebound books. The barcode, which includes the ISBN in digital form, is printed on the back cover. What do the numbers in the ISBN mean? Let's look at the ISBN for this book. It is 978-1-878853-91-0. The first two digit groups identify the series as a Bookland EAN ISBN number. The third and longest series of digits is unique to the publisher. Every ISBN of my company, Williams & Company, Publishers, contains these numbers. This means that anywhere, any time, any book bearing this series of numbers can be quickly identified as having been published by my company. Every publishing house has its own identifying numbers. This is known as the "publisher's prefix." The second to last group of digits identifies a specific title. No other title published by my company, for instance, bears the 91 signature. The last number is called a check digit. It is calculated in a complex way by manipulating the numbers that precede it. If the check digit is not what the computer says it should be, then there are errors in the rest of the ISBN.

When you have an ISBN you will be listed in Books In Print, the international database of published works. Without an ISBN you are invisible. Self-publishers should always get their own series of ISBN numbers and not use one furnished by another company.

Q. What is a book packager?

A. A book packager provides a variety of services for a client who seeks help in getting a book project organized and completed. He provides the needed services to complete the transition from book idea to ready-to-publish book. The extent of provided services varies widely from project to project.

• The packager may come up with and idea, find a freelancer to write it for him, and present the idea to the publisher.

• More likely, Sam, the book packager, will get a call like this from a publisher: "Sam, we need a beach-and-intrigue page turner for the next summer season." Sam says OK, comes up with a plot idea likely to satisfy, finds a writer, does a promo package and goes back to the publisher for final approval. The novel Jaws was created in this way.*

• Or Sam may prefer to work with individuals, say a plastic surgeon who wants to develop a reputation for himself. He tells Sam he wants to be the author of a best-selling book called "Look Ten Years Younger in Ten Days." Sam doesn't guarantee the best-selling part, but does find a suitable ghost writer and publisher for the doctor's book.

• Sam could prefer to work with self-publishers—as I do—helping them write for the market, edit and design a professionally attractive book, and set up their own publishing companies to sell it.

Q. What are "returns?"

A. Returns are the bane of the book business and a hotly debated topic today. Simply put, no book sales made to distributors, wholesalers or bookstores is final. If the book does not sell, these vendors can simply return unsold copies to the publisher for credit. For this reason small publishers take a financial risk they can scarcely afford when they shell out five or six thousand dollars to print enough books to fill a big order from a chain of bookstores. If the book lingers on the shelves more than a few weeks or months, the stores will return them and demand their money back. The publisher is left holding the financial bag. The so-called "right of return" dates from the 1930's, when cash was scarce and booksellers had little capital to invest in inventory. This device made acquiring inventory a kind of consignment arrangement in which the bookstore had no risk. Today, returns are a growing problem in the publishing industry, with some smaller publishers now refusing to agree to take back unsold inventory. But if you expect to do much business with the larger bookstores, there is noting you can do avoid accepting returns as a cost of doing business. Bookstores will not order books from publishers on a non-returnable basis

Q. I have written a children's book. What is the market for these?

A. The publication of books for children is a highly specialized niche market within the publishing business. To succeed in it requires a thorough knowledge of the market. There is a good deal of study and reading to do I recommend that you start with *The Business of Writing for Children*, by Aaron Shepard (Shepard Publications, $10) It is available at Amazon. Com. Shepard is a very talented and very practical man who will give you the real skinny on the topic. He says of his book: "Writing books for children is both art and business. If you dream of becoming a children's author—or even if you're well on your way—this handbook can help you in writing sale-able stories, getting them published, and promoting your books. Topics include common myths about children's writing, children's book categories, elements of successful stories, manuscript format, submission strategies, contract negotiation, the publishing process, career building, and children's writer resources. Also included are specialized subjects such as querying for multiple manuscripts, promoting a first book, and designing a Web page." Another highly recommended book for orientation to the children's market is *The Complete Idiots Guide to Writing Children's Books*, by Harold D. Underdown, an experienced editor and author of children's books. His web site, http://www.underdown.org/cig.htm, has a fine resource section

The specialized requirements for the genre are many. When you write for children you must be aware of vocabulary restraints for various ages, subject matter needs and taboos, typical lengths, etc.

There are various levels children's books. *Board books* are intended for first books for toddlers to look at an play with; *picture books* are intended to be read to, then by, somewhat older children; *concept books* teach children their colors, numbers, etc.; *easy readers* look more like normal books but are designed for beginning readers to read on their own; *chapter books* bridge the various levels between easy readers and *young adult books*. As a writer/self-publisher breaking into this market you need to target your book precisely to one of these groups. An inspection trip to a bookstore with a well-stocked children's section is a good first step in building your knowledge base. You can also go to www.write4children.com.

Q. I published a Ebook but have not sold any. Is there a problem?

A. You are a member of a fairly large club, as Ebook sales, with very few exceptions, remain limited. There are three kinds of obstacle that Ebooks must overcome in the marketplace before sales will increase:

1. *Technical limitations*: A serious limitation is the lack of any standard format for Ebooks. Adobe PDF, the front runner, and the format that I will use until some standardization comes along, is read mainly on personal computers. The hand-held devices often have proprietary formats of their own. Some programs, such as Microsoft Reader, are attempting to provide cross-platform accessibility to Ebooks, but

without too much success so far. The market for Ebooks will continue to be quite limited until a cross-platform format on a universal reader is accepted and implemented. When that happens, though, the Ebook phenomenon is likely to expand rapidly.

2. *Limitations due to negative perceptions of the marketplace*: books are not reviewed by main stream media and are, for the most part, not yet considered serious literary efforts.

3. *Limitations due to lack of visibility*. When you publish an Ebook how is one to know what it is about, that it is available, and where it is available. Tucked away on web sites, they are viewed by far too few readers to create meaningful demand. An Ebook, by its very nature, is invisible. A blockbuster title, at present, is the key to any hope of marketing success, and it must be a stroke of great marketing. Since the title is all most people will see of your book unless they sort through the pages of a web site to find a table of contents or a paragraph or two of sample contents, the title must be dramatic and possess great pulling power.

These are the limitations of Ebooks as I see them. The *New York Times* agrees that these limitations are serious. In a September, 2001, article writer David Kirkpatrick reports that "the main advantage of electronic books appears to be that they gather no dust. Almost no one is buying. Publishers and online bookstores say only the very few best-selling electronic editions have sold more than a thousand copies, and most sell far fewer. Only a handful have generated enough revenue to cover the few hundred dollars it costs to convert their texts to digital formats." Things haven't changed much since then.

Q. I am told that a "niche market" book is easier to market and sell than a book of general interest, such as a novel. Why is that?

A. You can't hit the bull's eye if you don't have a target. When your potential readers are easily identifiable—by interest or by location—you can reach them more easily with your message and sell books to them. Say you wrote a historical novel. Sure, there are people who not only like historical novels but who read little else. I like them myself. But who are these people? Where do they live? How do you tell them about your book? The answer is that you can't easily do these things, because your readers don't form an easily identified, homogenous group.

Niche markets require such a group. Generally they consist of groups like the following:

1. *Individuals or businesses who have similar interests and needs*, and so are easily targeted and reached. (All dentists, say, or all internet marketing companies)

2. *Individuals or businesses in a limited geographical area*, and so easily targeted and reached. (All inhabitants of Savannah, Georgia, say, or Key West). Such groups on individuals constitute a niche. Write a book that will interest them and you can target your prospects and sell to them. If your book is a good one, and if your niche is large enough, it will be profitable. The more specialized your niche market the better off you are, so long as the market is large enough to generate the volume of sales that you need.

A niche market is important because it is manageable: you can easily get your mind around it, your pocketbook around it, and your hands around it. Every nook and cranny of it can be plowed and farmed, like a small, fertile plot of land. You can find more on niche markets at http://www.PubMart.com. Go to the "resources" page.

Q. I understand how niche marketing can work for non-fiction. But can it work for fiction and poetry?

A. I know of one niche market for fiction and poetry that has a chance of working: a niche based on geographical tie-ins in high-traffic, tourist locations that attract a continuing stream of vacationers and visitors (new customers every day!). Books occupying such a niche build the people, history and/or character of a specific locale into its plot structure.

Eugenia Price's very popular novel *Savannah* illustrates this kind of niche. This book is a combination historical novel and romance. It is a good, light read, and in its pages old Savannah, its people, places and history, come alive. Why is such a novel a good bet for you? Because if you can't find a major publishing house to bring it out you can easily publish it yourself. You can do this because the book passes the essential marketing test: it has the possibility of intensive sales in a limited geographical area.

A modest first edition of such a book can be sold in the city itself and surrounding areas. Had Price self-published she could easily have gotten her book into bookstores, tourist gift shops and specialty stores, hotel and motel paperback racks and point of purchase sales spots in restaurants. She could have done this in Savannah and also, to some degree, in Atlanta and other Georgia cities and towns. There would have been only a limited amount of travel involved, which she could have managed with ease. Further, in a tourist hot-spot like Savannah there would be an ever-renewable group of book buyers (tourists) to keep sales going month after month.

There are variations on this theme. One of these was very successful for my friend Carole Marsh, president of Gallopade International and the author of many books for young people. Carole has written several books for teens and pre-teens set in major theme parks and other tourist sites. Any location with a heavy traffic of young people with a few dollars of souvenir money in their pockets or the pockets of their parents is a good candidate for this publishing scenario. A large theme park in Carole's part of the county was Carowinds, on the border between the two Carolinas, just south of the city of Charlotte. Carole wrote a book that she called The Carowinds Mystery. There was a strong, continuing sale of this and similar books by Carole Marsh linked to other, highly frequented and colorful locations.

This kind of niche can even work for poetry. I have published books of poems that fit the category, and not only sold them, but sold enough of them to make a profit and pay royalties to the poet—a very rare feat indeed. Another poet recently showed me a group of poems set in the South Florida landscape. Some of them were very good, especially one called "Key West Cats." I told the writer that I would publish the book if she could put together thirty or so poems on a similar theme. I knew that such a book would sell many copies, over a long period of time, in tourist spots in Key West and to most libraries in Florida

Q. How much money will I make when my book is published?

A. Let's start with a crash course in the economics of publishing. Here's the bad news: with very few exceptions, nobody makes much money in publishing.

Here's the way the business works. The publisher brings out a book. He can sell it, say, for $18.95. If the publisher knows his stuff and gets the best prices available, he can get 1000 copies printed and bound for $3000, plus freight, or $3 a book. He will have paid a typesetter and cover designer $1500 to $2000. He has marketing costs, office overhead, billing expenses and distribution expense. The publisher then pays the wholesalers and distributors who sell his book 65% of the cover price. Thus, if he sells every copy available to him for sale (950, since 50 will have been mailed out for review) he will gross $6300. Of that $6300 he will lose $630 to bad debts and spoilage (10%), leaving $5670. Yet he has paid the printer $3000, the typesetter and cover artist $2000. He will allow 10% of the gross for general office expense and overhead. All of this totals $5630. The result: in the best of all possible worlds the publisher shows a gross profit of only $670, and that is before royalties and returns. (The subject of "returns" is covered elsewhere in this FAQ.) If your book is well-reviewed and goes back to press for additional printings, the publisher, who has already amortized some of his up-front costs, begins to make more money and so does the author.

So what is your share? The "standard" royalty used to be 10% of the cover price, but that is no longer the case. In the case of a trade paperback, your royalty is more likely to be ten or twelve percent of "monies actually received." This means that if the publisher receives 33% of an $18.95 item, your royalty will be ten to 12 percent of that fractional amount. Royalties on book club sales and "promotional" (the going term for discounted) sales will be even lower. So-called POD publishers like IUniverse are likely to offer much higher royalties, but since they sell very few books, your high percentage does not do you much good. Last time I looked, forty percent of nothing was still nothing. Whatever your royalties are, they will usually be paid out to you twice yearly, about 60 days after the contract-specified royalty period comes to a close.

Q. Surely there other ways to profit?

A. This is the good news. Yes, fortunately, there are many other ways to profit from publication.

   1. *As a published author or self-publisher, you enjoy valuable tax benefits and shelters.* You don't have to own oil wells in Oklahoma or vast real estate subdivisions to cash in on generous features of the tax code. Your little home office will do much of it for you. If you use this space only for your writing business you will be able to deduct a proportional (based on square footage) share of your rent or mortgage interest,

utilities, telephone and many other household expenses like insurance and maintenance. That can be a substantial deduction. Further, since you are a professional writer, all of the books and newspapers you buy or subscribe to become tax deductions on Schedule C, (Profit or Loss from Business or Profession). Much travel also becomes deductible. I go to Chicago or L.A. every year for the four-day annual publishers' trade show, Book Expo America. It's deductible. A trip to New York for the Small Press Book Fair? Deductible. The Maui Writer's Conference? Deductible. Run all this stuff by your tax preparer or accountant as you fill out your tax return.

2. *Professional recognition and promotion.* My first book was called *Mallarmé and the Language of Mysticism,* and it was published by the University of Georgia Press. It got good reviews, but was suitable only for university libraries and a few other scholars in my narrow literary field. I made exactly $279 in royalties. I remember the precise figure because that was the first royalty check I ever got. Hardly a great return on a year's work. However, I was promoted to Associate Professor and, not too long thereafter, to full professor. My salary was raised accordingly. Before I left the groves of academe ten years later to start my own publishing company, I estimate that I had made over $100,000 directly attributable to one book.

4. *Grants and fellowships.* Once your book comes out you are in that fine fellowship of the "published writer." This means that you can begin to apply for grants to attend workshops, seminars and all manner of special events. You can apply for jobs teaching memoir writing on cruise ships to the Mediterranean and Greece. If you market your new-found reputation correctly, you will surely get some of the things you ask for.

5. *Secondary profit centers.* Based on your reputation as a published writer, you can give seminars and sell consultant's services to others who want to learn how to do what you have already done: get

published. You can do ghost writing, editing, business writing. These are many other profitable doors will be open to you once you begin to look for them.

Q. I am a self-publisher and my book is already published. Can I still make a deal with book clubs?

A. Yes, you can, if your book is not out of date. Look through the list of book clubs in Literary Market Place (available in your library reference room) and in the Publisher's Resource section of the Midwest Book Review web site (http://www.execpc.com/~mbr/). Find a club that offers books in the niche that your book falls into. Send them a query to ask if they would like to see a copy. Your deal with a book club will bring you an immediate chunk of cash from the initial purchase of books (very heavily discounted, but still profitable) and usually a later check for royalties on books sold. An example: I placed a book with one of the Doubleday Book Clubs. They purchased 1500 copies at $2 above actual production costs. This bought in a gross profit of $3000. I later received a check for royalties on books they had sold.

Q. Will my book be in bookstores?

A. "Bookstore" now means, for all practical purposes, the chains: Barnes & Noble, Borders, Books-a-Million, etc. There are a few regional chains, but one-by-one they are succumbing to the competition of the superstores. Oxford Books of Georgia recently bit the dust. In North Carolina, where I used to live, two regional chains were Wills Books and the Intimate Bookshops. Both are ow defunct. Many authors and self-publishers who come to my seminars seem to believe that newly published books automatically appear on bookstore shelves, as though they jumped into cardboard boxes all by themselves and shipped themselves out to the local Barnes & Noble. Nothing could be less true.More than 200,000 new books come out in the United States each year. There is room for only the smallest fraction of this number on bookstore shelves.

Smaller publishers submit their new titles to the buyer in the national office of the chains charged with deciding whether or not to carry a book. Bookstore buyers carefully evaluate new books to decide whether or not they are likely to turn a profit. They look at book design, price, competing titles, content and other factors to make their decisions. My publishing company, Williams & Company, Book Publishers, has had titles accepted and titles refused. All of them were, in our opinion, solid commercial products and were well-reviewed. The chains disagreed. They gave no explanation. Fortunately, we had other ways to sell such books. Many subsidy publishers assure authors that their books will be "available" in major bookstores nationwide. But "available" does mean "on the shelves." It simply means that if a customer goes to the help desk and asks for it, the clerk there will be able to look your book up in the Books-in-Print database and put in a special order. In such a situation the customer has to have heard of your book, or even seen it elsewhere, and decided that he or she wishes to purchase it. But you and I know that most of our bookstore purchases come as the result of a reader browsing the shelves. So simple "availability" is not much of an advantage. It is the books on the shelf that are going to be bought.

Q. My book was in bookstores for a while, but now I can't find it on the shelves. What's going on?

A. As hard as it is to get on those shelves, this is not the whole challenge. The trick is to stay there and see that your friendly UPS man does not grace your door with box after box of untold returns. When Barnes & Noble or another of the big chains has decided to stock your book and has neatly shelved it in the appropriate section of their stores, the number crunchers go to work. In two or three months' time these people will decide whether or not to keep your book there.

How is this done? Do they ask a literary critic whether your novel is great literature? Do they ask whether your how-to book is a truly important contribution to its field. Do they ask whether your slim volume of poetry is going to usher in a new age of creativity and insight? No, they do not. These super citizens of the bean-counting world know to the last inch how much shelf space exists in their stores, and they know to the last cent how much revenue each of those inches must produce annually if their store is going to be profitable. They know how much precious space your books consume and how many of them have been sold daily, weekly and monthly since they were put on display. The key question for them is not "Is this a good and worthy book?" but "Does this product produce a cash flow consistent with our financial goals?" If you don't measure up, zap! You're gone. Your books are quickly packed up and shipped back to your wholesaler, your distributor, and then back to you. Continue to do everything you can to get visibility for your book and stimulate buyers to go into bookstores and buy it.

Q. Who sets up the book tours/promotional tours and who pays for those expenses? Does the writer have any input to encourage the publishing house to spend more money to promote the book?

A. Only books that show signs of selling in big numbers will attract the marketing resources to finance a book tour. For first-time authors and self-published authors there will be no tour unless the lightning of best-sellerdom somehow strikes the book they have written. This can happen, but I would not stand out in the rain waiting for it. The only tours you are likely to have are the ones you set up yourself. If you are going to be traveling or vacationing in an metropolitan area, contact the community relations or special events coordinator in area bookstores and make a pitch for yourself and your book. Convince them that you can draw a crowd and put on a good show, and they may try to fit you in.

Q. What does it mean when a publisher declares a book "out of print?"

A. An out-of-print book is one that a publisher has decided to stop reprinting and stop selling. When this happens—as it frequently does—copies left on hand are sold to remainder dealers for a dime on the dollar or less. These are the "bargain books" that you see stacked on sales tables in bookstores. Sometimes leftover books are first offered to the author, who may purchase them and continue to sell them on his or her own. For someone who did this see the web site of Shel Horowitz (http://www.frugalfun.com). Horowitz purchased and continued to sell the remainders of his book, *The Penny-Pinching Hedonist*. Whether you have the chance to buy your book from the publisher may depend on the terms of your contract. Usually all rights automatically revert to an author when a book goes out of print. Exactly how and when this will happen should be covered in your original contract. At that time the license you granted to the publisher to sell your book will have ended, and you may do with it what you will.

Q. Can Ebooks and digtitally produced print-on-demand books go "out-of-print?"

A. Technically, an Ebook cannot go out of print.since it is never printed at all. In the case of print on demand, books are printed only in single copies to fill specific orders. This fact creates serious problems for writers who may be anxious for rights to revert back to themselves from the publishing company, and to date it these problems have not been definitively solved. In more traditional times in book publishing, contracts contained a clause specifying that rights would revert to the author when the book was sold out and the publisher chose not to reprint within a specified period, say 12 months. But now, with print-on-demand books, publishers who do not want to relinquish rights can claim that the a book is still "in print" in the digital format although no print version exists in their warehouse (or anywhere else). It exists only in the printers data base. This is just one area of writer/publisher relations that must be resolved now that Ebook and POD publishing have become commonplace. See the website of the National Writers Union (http://www.nwu.org) for a discussion of this and other problems.

Q. What are the most important points that should be (or should have been) covered in my author/publisher contract?

A. Publisher's contracts are thorny documents for unwary and inexperienced writers to work through. Contracts should always be read carefully and thoroughly. If you see a clause that you do not understand, ask for clarification. Often, publishers are quite willing to discuss contract terms you find objectionable, though they don't always change their minds. Some terms and conditions can have serious, unforeseen and very negative consequences for the writer. Here are some items I carefully review when contracts are offered to me:

1. The amount of the author's royalty on each copy sold and especially the method used in calculating this royalty. Is it based on the retail price, "monies actually received," or some other system.

2. An "escalation clause" which specifies the degree to which royalties increase as sales numbers grow. This usually takes the form of one royalty rate for the first XXX number sold, with additional increases as various, defined, sales plateaus are reached after that. What about new editions? Do the hard-earned escalation increases continue to build or do they fall back to zero?

3. When royalties are to be paid.

4. The amount of the advance. Is it refundable? (It should not be). When and how is it paid. The typical agreement pays the author a portion the advance on the signing of the contract and the balance on completion and approval of the manuscript.

5. The term of the contract. When (and how) will it end?

6. What happens to rights when the contract ends?

7. Date of publication

8. How many free copies will you get? How much will you have to pay for additional copies? A fifty percent discount in case lots is the best I personally have been able to get a publisher to agree to.

9. Do you give the publisher "first refusal" on your next book? If you do, specify how long he has to make up his mind.

11. What happens if the ms. is unacceptable to the publisher? If this is the case, it may be because your book is no longer, in the publisher's opinion, timely; because he has found another on the same theme he likes better; or simply because he is short of cash. It is not usually a question of quality, since he has already seen three or four chapters of your book prior to offering you a contract.

Since I am not a lawyer, I can't and don't give legal advice. But I can point you in the right direction. To learn more about publishing contracts and the perils and pitfalls that abound within them read Levin's book, *How to Be Your Own Literary Agent* (Ten Speed Press). You will find a detailed and very valuable analysis of publishing contracts there. Also check out the web sites of Ivan Hoffman, an attorney experienced in publishing law (http://www.ivanhoffman.com), and to the web site of the National Writer's Union (http://www.nwu.org). Both sites have much freely available information on publishing contracts.

Q. What goes into pricing a book? How do I know that the price is not too high or too low?

A. There are people out there who will tell you that there is some mathematical formula that you must follow: seven times the production cost; ten times the production cost; twelve times, etc. But such a formula doesn't always make a lot of sense. It is not even clear what is meant by "production cost." The bottom line is that, in coming up with a price, you have to juggle two numbers: (1) the least you can get by with and still make a profit and (2) The most that the market will bear. Somewhere between those two numbers you will find the optimum price for your book. Here are some things to keep in mind:

1. If a book buyer can get a book of the same scope and quality as yours at a lower price, he will go for the lower price every time. This, as students in Economics 101 will tell you, is known as the law of substitution. When I go to the newsstand and just want a couple of mystery novels to read while my wife is out of town and find that there are several good ones priced at $7.95 and two or three at $9.95 there's little hesitation. It's $7.95 every time.

2. However, if I am pricing a how-to manual on, say, how to start a city magazine, and there is only one of them out there, I will pay whatever the cover price is, within reason. I want and need the information. The information is in the book. So I buy the book. I published such a book on my web site (http:/www.PubMart.com), *Kitchen-Table Publisher: How to Make $100,000 a Year with Your Own Home-Based Publishing Company*, for some time at $59.95 and doing well with it. This book tells, step-by-step, how to publish city and regional magazines, newcomer guides, weekly newspapers, tabloids, shoppers, tourism guides and other publications. So far as I know it is the only book of its kind currently on the market. If there were similar books I would undoubtedly have had to lower my price.

3. If your book is the kind that has a good chance of a very high vol-

ume in sales, you can make a small profit on each of book sold and still do quite well.

4. If you have a niche market book with limited sales potential, you will have to set a higher price—otherwise the whole project is not worth your while.

5. If you sell your books directly on the internet you can experiment with pricing, trying this price this month and that price the next. For instance, I plan to offer my publishing manuals at a very substantial price reduction. If sales double or triple, I will make less on each sale but a great deal more overall. If sales remain the same, I will go back to the higher price.

Q. What makes a book sell?

A. There are three things and three things only that make most books sell: published reviews, individual reviews (word of mouth) and the SOB factor.

Published reviews in major publications like *Publishers Weekly, Library Journal*, and metropolitan newspapers are most sought after, but mini-reviews that consist of a mention by some specialty columnist can be ever better. The SOB part is the "Sweat of the Brow" of the author who works relentlessly to promote his book—anywhere and everywhere. He will send reviews and PR to every trade publication, weekly and community newspaper, shopper, special interest newsletter he can locate. He will scour every resource; give readings in every bookstore he can find; write supporting articles for every available magazine -- in short, do whatever it takes to sell books.

Q. Will my book be reviewed?

A. Good books looking for reviews swamp the offices of editors and publishers across the country all day, every day. Entire metropolitan landfills could be filled with this stuff. This slush makes it all the harder for any particular writer or publisher to rise above the rubble and get noticed. At the same time, the space devoted to book reviews is shrinking day-by-day. More and more metropolitan newspapers are dropping their weekly book review inserts and others are reducing the number of column inches devoted to books in their regular Arts and Leisure sections. With mail bag after mail bag coming in every week, you have about ten seconds — at most — to get singled out for possible review. A big city daily receives hundreds of books every week and mentions maybe four or five of them. Not very good odds. So send your books to more fertile fields: specialty columnists in other sections of the paper and magazines; weekly papers across the county (which may even publish the canned reviews you send out with or without a copy of your book); radio stations; community service people; professional journals, etc.

Make sure to send a fact sheet on you and the book, a short-short article about it and a feature story of no more than 500 words along with every review copy of your book that you send out. Some of these will be published.

Q. What are the most common reasons that a book fails to be reviewed?:

A. Here's my personal list of reasons why a book fails to get reviewed:

1. It falls off the reviewer's desk and doesn't get noticed.

2. It is ugly to look at.

3. The subject is not of general interest.

4. The person assigned to review the book went on vacation and never submitted the review.

5. The first paragraph was not strong enough to keep the reviewer reading. Remember, the job of the first paragraph is to entice the

reader to continue on to the second one, and so on through the book.

6. It was scheduled for review, but the publication ran out of space.

7. Plain bad luck.

The following is a list of no-review reasons developed by Jim Cox, editor of the *Midwest Book Review*:

1. The book was not submitted according to the submission guidelines and preferences of a particular Book Review. For example, galleys were sent when only the finished books are considered—or finished books were sent when only galleys are considered.

2. The book subject was inexpertly handled by the author.

3. The cover is amateurish in its design

4. The first paragraph is not well written. Even when in rare cases when someone does pick up your book and turn to the opening page, the first paragraph or two does not bode well for the quality of the rest of the book.

5. Insufficient information was included with the book to complete a review (I can't tell you how often a price is missing, there is no publisher address, 800 numbers and even addresses were left off, no publicity release accompanied the book, etc., etc., etc

5. Space/time limitations.

Q. How Do I Get on Radio and TV

A. Do two things:

1. Reach the primary decision maker.

2. Offer that decision maker something that he or she thinks will be good for their show.

The larger the market the show reaches, the more difficult these two things become. If, after your book is published, everybody is talking about it, everybody is reviewing it, and there is general and widespread excitement about it, then you may — repeat, may — stand a very slim chance of getting on Oprah or one of the biggies. But I wouldn't want to go without bread and water until it happened. Still, there are other show-time opportunities that will be open to you. It takes a little know-how and a lot of persistence to cash in on them. Here are some pointers:

1. Send an "available for interview" info form and a cover letter to talk show hosts on radio and TV in your immediate area. This form will include a brief bio on you, a bit about what is in your book and why listeners will be interested in it, and some sample questions you are prepared to answer—all of this is geared toward helping your radio/TV interviewer achieve *his or her* goals by helping you achieve yours. Follow up with a telephone call. If your communication did not reach the right person, find out who the right person is and send out your info again. Keep a record of whom you have contacted, and when, and the results. Try again at regular intervals.

2. Never forget that PR is a two-way street. You have give to get. Always do the following three things to the best of your ability::

—Provide a hook. Tell the show host what will your interview do to pull in listeners and viewers.

— Whenever appropriate, tell how you and your book will help provide solutions for problems shared by many listeners.

— If your topic becomes relevant to hot news of the day, fax a press release to your target decision maker immediately.

There are some web sites that connect authors and experts with media people looking for good interview prospects. One of them is Lorilynn Bailey's *Guestfinder* site, at http://www.guestfinder.com.

Q. How can I get ready for an interview? I haven't done one before and I am nervous about it.

A. Preparation is the key. To be prepared is to be at ease. Here are a few tips.

1. Make a list of questions you would like to be asked. Give this list to the host before you go on the air.

2. Insofar as possible, cater to the interviewer's own interests

3. Have an easy way for listeners to buy a book or contact you, and let them know about it. Name a specific local bookstore.

4. Be active rather than passive. Answer the questions you wish you had been asked, whether they are actually asked or not.

5. Start with an anecdote. "Let me tell you what happened to me up in Yeehaw Junction. . . ."

6. Address your host by his or her first name

Q. Won't it cost a lot of money to travel all over the country just to get on a radio show?

A. Radio interviews are done by telephone. Here's what the editors of Radio-TV Interview Report (http://www.rtir.com) had to say about on this subject: "You can appear on talk shows without traveling all across the country. Most radio stations will interview you via telephone from the comfort of your home or office. Imagine speaking to audiences in Boston, Miami, New York and Phoenix all in the same day, just by doing phone interviews with radio stations!"

Q. How do I know if I'm doing enough to market my book?

A. I could say that you'll know you've done enough when you've sold them all. But even then, you'll just go back for a reprint and start selling all over again.

I firmly believe in what I call the "Rule of Five," which I learned from Al Canton of Adams-Blake Publishing Company. "Don't let the sun set," Al says, "before you have come up with and implemented five new ways to promote your book. Every day, five ways, no exceptions."

Where to get ideas for promotion? Keep a notebook with you at all times to jot down ideas that will come to you at random. Some of your best ideas will come this way and will be lost unless you make note of them. Consult John Kremer's *1001 Ways to Promote Your Book.* This book is a rich source of promotional ideas. You may not accept any of them word for word, but I promise you that just browsing through will suggest other ideas that will be valuable to you.

Q. Do I have to get my book translated to sell foreign rights?"

A. You do not have to translate your book before you sell foreign rights. If a publisher in a foreign country buys rights to your book, that publisher will find a translator. That's the way it works.

Q. Why does it take so long to get a book published?

A. It takes a long time because there are so many things to do. In fact, it is generally bad news if a book is published too quickly. It usually means that all the prepublication marketing has not taken place. Here's what happens: First your book is edited; then it is typeset and proofed; then proofed again; then portions of the book are sent out for the promotional quotes (blurbs) that you see on the back page; then, three months or more before the official publication date, galleys are sent to major review sources such as *Publisher's Weekly, Library Journal* and a few others appropriate to your subject matter. Next, book clubs may be approached about featuring your book as a monthly main or alternate selection. All of this will take six to twelve months. It is hard to see how this period of time can be shortened without risking negative results for the book in question.

Q. Who owns the copyright, me or my publisher?

A. Except in cases where your contract states explicitly that your book is a "work made for hire" you, as writer and creator of the work, own the copyright. The publishing contract simply gives the publisher license to print and sell your book under the terms and for the time specified by your contract.

Q. What if there are typographical errors in my book?

A. Typographical errors and careless misspellings and certainly blemishes to avoided by every available means, one does find errors in most books these days. Always correct such errors in a second printing. Here's a story to give you courage. I am reading a biography of E.B. White. White spent his life writing for the New Yorker, and he was fastidious with words. He published the little *Manual of Style* that you so often see recommended. In the introduction to the book, the biographer, Scott Elledge, is talking about the clarity and precision of White's style. In that very paragraph there are two glaring typographical errors, the only two I found in the book. So here's my take on typos: Learn to live with them. A few always seem to get through the editorial net. Don't stress out over them. Just correct them at the first available opportunity.

Q. I see the names of the same writers in my local newspaper over and over again. Why does everyone keep overlooking me?

A. Many of us share this feeling. We wonder why the names of the same writers seem to appear in local and regional anthologies, magazines and small press reviews over and over again; why the same people are always appointed to arts commissions, asked to give talks and write introductions, participate in arts festival programs, get appointed to state arts posts, and give talks to yearly writers group meetings. It's not a matter of luck, nor is it a plot that these names appear so frequently. It's just that these people have managed, one way or another, to create a public visibility adequate to build a literary reputation. You can do he same. When organizers or grant givers fish around for the name of a "writer" for some purpose or other, they naturally choose among those that they have heard about. How could they do otherwise? What you've got to do is make sure that next time, they will have heard of you, if you want to achieve this higher level of visibility in the literary world, you must let people know who and what you are. It is time to blow your own horn a little. There is no ostentation here, no unjustified self-aggrandizement. It is just a matter of telling the truth and taking the simple and gentle steps of self-promotion that will insure public recognition of your success as a writer. For more, see the chapter "The Unabashed Poet's Guide to Self-Promotion" in my book *Poet Power!* (Sentient Publications).

Q. You talk about news releases. What is a news release, and how do you write one? Is it OK to write one for yourself?

A. It's not only OK to write a news release for yourself, but usually necessary that you do so. All the other writers you know are busy sending out their own releases. You do have to follow a simple, objective journalistic form. Your release can often be as brief as a single paragraph about the publication of your new book or a talk that you are going to give at a book fair, at a book signing at a local book store. You send this paragraph to newspapers big and small, newsletters, arts-oriented radio and TV (NPR) and any other media you can think of in hope of publication. Sometimes your release can be long as two or three hundred words (these had better be good) long. Long releases generally have an important reader information hook. If you have written a book on budget-priced vacations, write your release with a strong how-to slant, mentioning yourself and your book as part of the background. The more you're able to combine your own interest in generating publicity with the publication's interest in printing good stories, the more likely you are to get your released published.

News releases are mailed, faxed or emailed (I do both) to all publications that could conceivably be interested in it. Larger newspapers may pick up a bit here and there, or in rare cases, have a reporter call to do a story. Smaller newspapers such as community weeklies depend on well-written news releases to fill their pages, so your chances or getting your material published are much better with them. Be sure to write your release in an ego-free, newspaper-friendly style. Your object is not to tell people how great you are but to get your name out in front of them and let them draw their own conclusions.

Many books will tell yo how to write news releases, including my own publishing manuals (http://www.PubMart.com). Paul Krupin as written a fine manual called *Trash-Proof News Releases* (http://www.trashproofnewsrelease.com) that I highly recommend.

Q. Can news releases really help?

A. No doubt about it. Here's a story I tell in my how-to publishing manual, *Kitchen-Table Publisher*. I was starting a new company to publish city magazines. We needed a line of credit, but it was a time of tight money, and the banks didn't want to venture out on the limb as far as we needed them to. I began to send out a regular stream of news releases. These were brief notices of three or four sentences, meant to be published in the business notes section of our newspaper. One told how we planned a new city magazine in another town. A second told how we had hired a new "Executive Vice president" (in reality a salesman) to handle our Raleigh, North Carolina office (his car and a motel room). A third told how we planned three more magazines (that we had not yet published) and so on. Two months later I went back to my banker. "I hear you guys are going great guns," he said, smiling as he shook my hand. And he offered me the line of credit I needed. Similarly, when the president of the Arts Council is looking for a writer to do a keynote address for the upcoming book fair, the newspaper stories about you and your writing will come to mind and you will be in the running for the job.

Q. What is a "media kit," and do I need one?

A. Every writer needs a media kit. It is your essential tool to getting the media exposure that you need both to sell your books and to develop your reputation so that you can access the perks and secondary profit centers that will come your way as a writer. The following is an except from my book, *Poet Power! The Poet's Complete Guide to Getting Published* describing what a writer's media kit should contain. Although written for poets, the excerpt applies to all working writers. Your media kit should contain the following items. You may not use all of them every time you send a kit out, but you should have all of them available.

1. A fact sheet on yourself as author. This fact sheet will include a short bio of you, a listing of your credits, short excerpts from favorable reviews or interviews, a statement of your goals and motivations as a writer, quotable quotes, etc. Present these materials in an easily utilized, outline form so that a feature writer or reviewer can find and excerpt materials that are needed for a write-up.

2. In preparing this fact sheet, as in preparing all the other marketing materials in your repertoire, bear in mind that reporters—whether print or electronic—will not have time to research an article on you

and your work. You have to do this for them. When your fact sheet is well done and easily utilized you take a giant step toward getting the kind of publicity you need. The fact sheet can also be used as a background piece to include in your poetry submissions to magazines and to publishers. It can be given to program chairmen who have to introduce you to audiences before whom you are scheduled to appear. You can have it blown up to poster size and use it as a prop at readings, autograph parties, and other occasions.

3. Your media kit will also include a fact sheet on your book. What press published it? How many pages? What about special themes? What about quotes to illustrate these themes? How can the book be obtained? At what price? Your book fact sheet may well include an item or two that also appears on your personal fact sheet. Don't worry about necessary duplication but don't repeat materials needlessly.

4. Clips of any pre-publication or other reviews (or interviews) that you may have had. You will photocopy these and keep them readily available.

5. Copies of any other articles that may have been written about you or by you.

6. A brief news release of one full page or less, a short, straightforward note telling that you wrote your book and that it was published.

7. A complete feature article of 500 to 700 words, with photographs. This piece is a personality profile of you and your work. Will the article be used? Sometimes it will and sometimes it won't. It all depends on the space availability and intrinsic interest of your article. One thing, though, is certain. It will certainly not be used if you do not write it and send it out. Most newspapers are understaffed and do not have a regular book review editor. Some writers will use your article as a guide. Some newspapers—especially weeklies, which will be happy to have a free feature—will print it just as you provide it.

Always manage to tell readers how and where they can buy your book. Include a mention of your publishing company: "My Book of Poems was published by Muse Books of Tupelo, Mississippi." Also include a mention of the retail price.

8. Include a glossy, black and white photograph of yourself if you think there is any chance of its being used. An action shot in a natural surrounding will get a better play than a simple mug shot because it will have greater reader interest.

Q. I am told that I need a "sell sheet" or a information sheet on my book. What is this? What does it include?

A. I mentioned the fact sheet in item three of the media kit answer, above. Here are some more details. Your book fact sheet or sell sheet should contain the following items, on a single page.

1. *A reproduction of the cover of your book*, in thumbnail size. You can create this on your scanner and import the image into your page layout program.

2. *The title of your book, ISBN, page count, price, specifications (hardcover, trade paper, etc.).*

3. *The author's name*

4. *The publisher.* If you are a self-publisher, put the imprint you have chosen for your publishing company in this space.

5. *Publisher address, phone number, email address, website.*

6. *The name of the person to contact for further information.*

7. *A one or two paragraph descriptive summary* or bulleted list of chief points covered.

8. *A one paragraph author bio.*

Q. I know my book is good and solid. Why isn't it selling?

A. Good books can fail to sell for many reasons. Here are some of the most common ones.

1. *Physical reasons*: This category includes poor, amateurish cover and interior design that violate all the principles of good design practice. This is a frequent problem with self-published books.

2. *The market is too limited.* Perhaps you published a niche market book with two few individuals in that niche.

3. *The market is there but you can't get you message to them.* Markets that are too diffuse, widespread on not easily identified can be difficult and expensive to reach (to the point of being prohibitive for small publishers and self-publishers.

4. *The book is not timely.* Successful topical books ride the wave of public interest. Once the wave of interest is gone the market for the book is gone, too. I recently had a book submitted to me by an elderly woman who, as a young school teacher, had spent time at Berkely University during the flower-child sixties. She had a well-written memoir which I would once have considered publishing, but I rejected her book. Time had passed the subject by.

5. *The book is priced incorrectly.* Never forget the rule of substitution. If a buyer can find a cheaper product to do the same job as more expensive one, he will buy the cheaper one. If your book is priced to high, others will be substituted for it. But books can also be priced too low. When booksellers, wholesalers and distributors get their cut of the retail price pie, there may not be enough left over for the publisher pay his overhead and continue to market the product.

Q. Are there any professional organizations I can join that will help me understand the publishing business and market my books?

A. Yes, there are a number of them.

    1. The National Writers Union (http://www.nwu.com). The

National Writers Union is open to any writer who wishes to join. You will also find a great deal of useful information on the sale of rights on the National Writers Union web site . As I write this I have just visited their site and come up with the following list of publications for writers:

— Authors in the New Information Age: Electronic Publishing Issues.

—Standard Journalism Contracts and Handbook.

—NWU Guide to Book Contracts

—NWU Guide and Model Contract for Ghostwriting & Collaborations

—NWU Preferred Literary Agent Agreement and Understanding the Agent-Author Relationship

—NWU Guide to Fair Use

—Electronic Rights Policy

—Electronic Rights Negotiation Strategies

—Statement of Principles on Electronic Books

—Recommended Principles for Contracts Covering Online Book Pub lishing

—Technical Writers Code of Practice (Hardware/Software Industries)

2.The American Society of Journalists and Authors (http://www.ASJA. org)

3. Independent Publishers Association (formerly the Publishers Marketing Association) Access their website at http://www.PMA.com.

4. The National Writers Union and the American Society of Journalists and Authors maintain web sites that contain a great of current information for members and non-members alike. I highly recommend them.

Index

A

anecdote 92
ATC factor 85
Atlantic Monthly 88
Atlantis 77

B

black hole theory of the mind 69ff
bookstore browser 86
Brande, Dorothea 87
Burns, Ken 79

C

Carnegie, Dale 95
category folders 66
Chad Hurley 79
Chen, Steve 79
Critias 77
Critique of Pure Reason 97

D

Denver Post 79
Descartes, René 97
details, importance of 88
dialogue 89
Discourse on Method 97
Duke University 78

E

Extra Sensory Perception 78
*Extra Sensory Perception after Sixty
     Years.* 78

F

folder 63ff

free association 71
freelancer's paradigm 92

G

Gentlemen's Quarterly 88
Get Paid to Write 65
Google 82
Grazer, Ben 76

H

Harlequin romance 75
Hill, Napoleon 118
Hoffman, Phyllis 93
*How to Win Friends and Influence
     People* 95
Hurley, Chad 79

I

ideas 76
idea slips, sorting of 63
intellectual capital 76

J

Johnson, Magic 80

K

Kant, Immanuel 97

L

Lewis, C.S. 74

M

Mecklenburg Gazette 91
mind-mapping 71ff

Mind-Mapping for Kids 71
Moore, Michael 79
Mother Earth News 88
Mount Parnassus 78

N

New Yorker 88

O

Oracle of Apollo 78

P

parapsychology 78
Parapsychology Institute 78
Peale, Norman Vincent 95
Peck 95
Hoffman, Phyllis 93
Plato 77
psychokinesis 78
Publishing for Entrepreneurs 94

Q

quotes, techniques for handling 89

R

Reader's Guide to Periodical Literature 81
Republic 77
Rhine, J.B. 78
Rhodes, Richard 98
Romeo and Juliet 75
Rose, M.J. 78
Rose, Pete 78

S

Salon 77
Scientific American 88
See You at the Top 95

self-criticism 70
Shakespeare 75
Southern Lady 93
Steve Chen 79
Stone, Clement 81
subheads 92
Success Through a Positive Mental Attitude 81, 95
Symposium 77

T

telepathy 78
The Onion 88
Think and Grow Rich 95
tone, inappropriate 88
transitional question 92

V

Vick, Michael 78
Vidimos, Robin 79

W

Wall Street Journal 88
Wayne Dyer 95
We Choose America 81
Who's Who in America 81

Y

YouTube 79

Z

Zig Ziglar 95

Printed in the United States
147034LV00004B/13/P